CW01239087

Achievements of Civilization

THE BOOK OF WEALTH
Book Six

WEALTH IN RELATION TO MATERIAL

and

Intellectual Progress and Achievement

BEING

An Inquiry into the Nature and Distribution of the World's Resources and Riches, and a History of the Origin and Influence of Property, its Possession, Accumulation, and Disposition in all Ages and among all Nations, as a Factor in Human Accomplishment, an Agency of Human Refinement, and in the Evolution of Civilization from the Earliest to the Present Era

BY

HUBERT HOWE BANCROFT

NEW YORK

THE BANCROFT COMPANY, PUBLISHERS

1896

THE BOOK OF WEALTH was first published in 1896 by Hubert Howe Bancroft

This updated "Popular" edition published 2014 by BancroftBookofWealth.com

Prepared for publication by John R. Cumbow

Cover design, book layout and additional material
copyright © 2014 by John R. Cumbow
All rights reserved

THE BOOK OF WEALTH – Popular Edition – Book Six

ISBN-10: 1479341398
ISBN-13: 978-1479341399

www.BancroftBookofWealth.com

THE BOOK OF WEALTH – Popular Edition

Publisher's Note:

Originally published in 1896 in a special edition by Hubert Howe Bancroft, THE BOOK OF WEALTH consisted of 10 oversized volumes, bound in silk. The books were never intended for distribution to the general public. Only a few thousand copies were ever printed, and the books were marketed exclusively to the world's wealthiest families and individuals. Sold by subscription in strictly limited editions, the complete set was sold at that time for $2,500 — a very large sum of money even today!

More than 100 years old, the 10 volumes of THE BOOK OF WEALTH still offer valuable information for the modern reader. In order to make this rare set of books available to a wider audience, we are republishing the ten individual books in a modern 'Popular Edition' at a fraction of the original price.

Each of the books in our 'Popular Edition' includes the complete text from the original 'Fin de Siecle' edition published at the dawn of the 20th century. We've retained all of the original archaic language and spelling, as well as many of the engravings, line drawings and photogravures that illustrated the original volumes.

We trust that you, the modern reader, will find the contents of these rare books worthy of your attention.

NOTE OF CAUTION: Controversial even in his own time, Hubert Howe Bancroft's writings are not necessarily "politically correct." Some of his remarks could even be characterized as racist. That said, we feel it is important to include them here to present a more complete picture of the man and his times.

.

www.BancroftBookofWealth.com

THE BOOK OF WEALTH

BOOK SIX

CONTENTS

CHAPTER THE SIXTEENTH
GREAT BRITAIN AND IRELAND 3

CHAPTER THE SEVENTEENTH
AFRICA 59

CHAPTER THE EIGHTEENTH
AUSTRALIA, THE HAWAIIAN ISLANDS 85

RESOURCES 101

CHAPTER THE SIXTEENTH

GREAT BRITAIN AND IRELAND

Earth has not anything to show more fair;
Dull would be he of soul who could pass by
A sight so touching in its majesty:
This city now doth like a garment wear

The beauty of the morning: silent, bare,
Ships, towers, domes, theatres, and temples lie
Open unto the fields, and to the sky.
All bright and glittering in the smokeless air.

Never did sun more beautifully steep
In his first splendour valley, rock, or hill;
Ne'er saw I, never felt, a calm so deep!

The river glideth at his own sweet will:
Dear God! the very houses seem asleep;
And all that mighty heart is lying still!

— *Wordsworth's Lines on Westminster Bridge*

"BRITISH gold," said Napoleon I, "has often been a more potent factor in deciding the destiny of nations than the largest armies led by the ablest generals." Yet, except a few hundred ounces taken from low grade deposits in Wales, costing more than its value to extract, none of this metal has ever been mined in the British isles; while of silver, found in combination with lead, the average yield is less than 300,000 ounces a year. It is to her manufactures, as need hardly be said, and to the commerce mainly developed therefrom, that Great Britain owes her wealth, and apart from manufactures the nation would be one of the poorest on earth. That it is one of the richest is due, as the Briton would have us believe, to the superior intelligence, enterprise, and skill of British capitalists and British workmen. Is it not rather due to the fact that coal can be raised to the mouth of the pit for six shillings a ton? Yet the Englishman's self-conceit is not altogether inexcusable; for coal can be brought to the surface even at cheaper rates in the United States, in Germany, and in Belgium, though not in such close proximity to iron-beds, to navigable water, and to manufacturing centres.

In physical structure England has been described as "an epitome of the world's geology," nearly all existing formations, from the Silurian to the most recent of tertiary strata being found in this little sea-girt country, less than 60,000 square miles in area. Much of the shore line is gradually changing, the sea gaining on the land or the land encroaching on the sea, in some places as much as 30 feet in a year. In the county of Kent there is a tract of marsh land, some 25,000 acres in extent, which was once an arm of the sea, where vessels passed through deep water to ports no longer in existence. On the other hand there are many points, as on the Yorkshire coast, where the cliffs are slowly crumbling away, buildings disappearing from time to time with the solid earth that supports them.

The mountain system of England and Wales consists of one principal chain, but with innumerable ramifications, extending from the border of Scotland to the western extremity of Cornwall, whose towering cliffs present a bold front to the Atlantic. The highest of the system is Mount Snowdon in Wales, its summit easily accessible, though mist-wreathed almost throughout the year. Then there are Helvellyn, Scawfell, and "bold Skiddaw," standing guard over the lake region and all more than 3,000 feet in height, while in the Cheviot hills there are peaks from 2,000 to 2,500 feet above the sea level. Most of the larger rivers flow eastward, the Thames with its estuary draining an area of 10,000 square miles, the Trent and Ouse, whose streams unite in the Humber, carrying off the surface waters of an equal area, and the Severn, Mersey, and Avon ranking high among fifty or more navigable streams, to say nothing of smaller rivers and rivulets. The rainfall is ample but not excessive, except in a few localities, varying as a rule from 35 to 18 inches, though at certain points, as in the village of Beddgelert, near the foot of Snowdon, 50 or 60 inches are an average precipitation. The climate is moist and mild, with a mean annual temperature of about 50°, — in summer 60° and in winter 40° — the gulf-stream (by which alone is made habitable northeastern Europe), here first making itself felt on its eastward course from the land-locked cauldron of the gulf of Mexico.

SNOWDON MINES, WALES

The soil is moderately fertile, though adapted rather to pasturage than agriculture, except in the midland and southern counties, where with the use of fertilizing substances 40 bushels of wheat to the acre and 60 of oats or barley are no uncommon yield. In the useful minerals the country is rich, the annual output of coal averaging more than 175,000,000 tons; so that nearly all other industries are subsidiary to this potent factor in the production of wealth. Manufactures and commerce are, as I have said, on a stupendous scale, and in other respects Great Britain is a favored realm as compared with continental Europe. For the rich it is a pleasant land to dwell in, and for the poor it is one of the best, apart from the British colonies and the United States. Here can be had for money whatever money will purchase, and many things besides; pleasant environment, cultured if somewhat exclusive associates, and the most attractive of landscape scenery. There is nothing grand in English as there is in Scottish scenery; but there is much that is beautiful, verdure-clad hills alternating with fair and fertile valleys, woodlands with lush meadows, and heath-clad mountains and moors, bordering on the marge of loch or lake, forming one of the strongest elements of the picturesque.

In the Britain of early days, when Tyrian mariners visited her coasts to barter trinkets for tin and lead, there was nothing to indicate her future greatness, nothing even to make the land in anywise desirable as the abode of civilized man. As related by the Massilian traveller Pytheas, who wrote in the fourth century B.C., but of whose works quotations only remain, the island consisted almost entirely of forest and marsh, with a few openings in the woods in which cattle and sheep were pastured, and here and there a narrow strip near the shore, whose scant uncertain crop of grain was threshed in sheds and not on open floors; for there was little sunshine and almost perpetual rain. Caesar and Tacitus identify the inhabitants with the Iberians and Gauls, the interior being occupied by races which claimed to be indigenous, and the sea-coast by those who had come in search of booty or adventure. "The population," writes Caesar, "is numerous beyond all counting, and very numerous also the houses, resembling closely the dwellings of the Gauls. They have great numbers of cattle, and for money use copper, or copper coin, or bars of iron fashioned to a certain weight."

When Britain was finally reduced to a Roman province, guarded and garrisoned by Roman legions, industrial and commercial development followed rapidly in the train of conquest. The harvests became so abundant that a surplus was often available for shipment to other provinces; mines were opened, especially of iron, tin, and lead, and the remains of villas unearthed by archaeologists point to a condition of general prosperity. From Londinium, or London, which Tacitus describes about 60 A.D. as a thriving mart of trade, highways built in the solid Roman fashion, not a few of them in use to-day, radiated throughout the island, connecting with busy seaports, and thence with the system of communication which linked together the Roman world. When these roads were traversed by the emperor Hadrian, whose wall from the Solway Firth to the North sea, costing $5,000,000 in our present currency, was but a portion of his interminable line of border fortifications, many flourishing towns were already in existence. In the south, to use modern names only, were Canterbury and Winchester, Bath and Exeter; in the east were Norwich and Colchester, while Lincoln and Leicester, Gloucester and Chester were centres of municipal life, and from York a chain of villages extended almost to the Forth and the Clyde.

WATER TOWER AND ROMAN BATHS

But while subdued by Roman arms, Britain received no lasting impress from Roman arts, that language never superseding the Gaelic and giving place to the Germanic element, of which the Anglo-Saxon tongue is mainly composed, though as with the German itself containing a large number of words of Latin derivation. While the towns were romanized, it was not so with the farming communities whose dwellings clustered around the villas of wealthy Italian landowners; nor with those who lived apart from their conquerors, retaining their own language, institutions, and laws, as was permitted to all except men whose enforced labor was needed for farm or mine. Thus we must not overestimate the civilization of Britain during the Roman period, its condition resembling somewhat that of northern Russia in the present day, a country where man is still hewing his way through tracts of forest primeval, and where settlements are hardly sufficient to relieve the silence of nature's solitudes. Woodland, moorland, and morass covered nine-tenths of its surface, and except in a few localities, the clearings on river banks were the merest strips of cultivation threading their way through an extensive waste. There was nothing to encourage the romanization of Britain in the sense that Gaul and Spain were romanized; there was little natural wealth, or at least such wealth as was then available; and so great was the scarcity of precious metals that the moderate tribute of three thousand pounds of silver a year was collected with difficulty. No wonder that this, the last of the northern provinces subjugated by the Caesars was the first to be left to its fate.

In the history of Britain, two ages of authentic annals are separated by a long era of fable and tradition. Of Clovis and Charlemagne we know that they were at least historic personages, however their exploits may have been exaggerated; but Hengist and Horsa, Arthur and Mordred are beings the fact of whose existence is doubtful, and whose deeds and adventures must be ranked as to credibility with those of Ulysses and Aeneas. It was late in the third century that the channel pirates known as Saxons, belonging to a confederation of German tribes, began to make themselves felt, sailing swiftly from harbor to harbor in long, flat-bottomed boats, freighted with warriors and driven by fifty oars. Slave-hunting was the principal object of their raids, and this was attended with features even more repulsive than the modern slave-hunting of Arab traders. "Before setting sail homeward," continues Sidonius, "their wont is to slay by protracted and most painful tortures one man in every ten of those whom they have captured, in compliance with a religious custom which is even more lamentable than their superstitions."

At first the raids of the Saxons were confined to the shores of Gaul, and it was not until the year 364 that we hear of any organized attack on the coasts of Britain, though after this date their ravages were incessant. So long as the legions remained they caused but little damage; but these withdrawn, the country fell a ready prey to the invaders, while the Picts, after many former incursions, swarmed without check or hindrance over the Roman wall. In vain did Britain's chieftains appeal to Honorius to replace the troops. "The barbarians," they wrote, "drive us into the sea; the sea drives us back on the barbarians; and between them we know not what to do." But the legions were needed for the protection of more important provinces, and the emperor made answer that they must provide for their own defence. Imitating the policy by which Rome had hastened its doom while seeking to avert it, they attempted to hire as mercenaries for protection against the Picts the freebooters who harried their coasts, thus matching barbarian against barbarian. They came, not as mercenaries but as conquerors, and from these pirate hordes was developed in due time the Anglo-Saxon dynasty, or group of dynasties, somewhat in the manner following.

First among those who were drawn to Britain's shores by promises of land and pay was a band of Jute, or Jutish warriors, a tribe whose name is preserved in the word Jutland, though dwelling probably on the southern coast of Scandinavia, or in the Danish isles. They came, as the legend relates, "in three keels," and at their head were Hengist and Horsa, ealdormen, or aldermen, of the tribe. First setting foot on the isle of Thanet, near the chalk cliffs of the Kentish shore, at a spot where are now a few grey cottages saved from destruction by a sea-wall, after much hard fighting they presently subjugated what is now the county of Kent, with certain neighboring territory. But the latter they could not long retain; for before many years they were hemmed in on all sides by Saxon settlements, among them those of the Suthsexe and Eastsexe, these names being tribal and not territorial, as in the modern Sussex and Essex. In 495 the two Saxon ealdormen Cynric and

Cerdic founded a colony on what is now the coast of Hampshire, and their conquests spreading afar, a quarter of a century later they deemed themselves strong enough to assume the title of royalty. Here was the origin of the powerful kingdom of the Westsexe, or West Saxons, that is to say of the kingdom of England; for such in time it became.

While under Saxon, Jutish, and Anglian leaders, there were founded seven or eight principal kingdoms, with a large number of minor states, all later united in one, the heptarchy belongs to the traditions and not to the history of the period during which Britain was gradually transformed into England. By the close of the sixth century there were Saxon colonies at least as far north and west as the estuary of the Severn; but it was in the southern and southeastern districts that their settlements were most numerous; for here was a region waiting to be plundered, one filled with the homes of wealthy provincials long after the legions were recalled from Britain's shores. Thus it is that when the Saxons were fairly established in the country, we read of the costly furniture and appointments of their dwellings; their dishes of gold and silver, their tables and chairs elaborately carved and sometimes inlaid with the precious metals, their golden tissues and embroideries, and their silken and other tapestries ornamented with figures of birds and flowers.

In the village of Bignor in Sussex have been unearthed the remains of a country mansion belonging to the fifth century, which is thus in substance described by Wright in his *Wanderings of an Antiquary*. The several buildings enclosed a court more than a hundred feet square, with tessellated pavement, and on its inner side a covered colonnade. In the mansion itself, the hall with its central fountain was of the type which the Italians brought from their sunny land, the furnace which heated the banqueting-room showing that they knew how to accommodate themselves to the rigors of a northern climate. The floors of the larger chambers were of costly and elaborate mosaic work, and the walls were aglow with frescos, some fragments of which still retain their original brightness of color. In one of the apartments were figures of dancing nymphs; in another was portrayed the rape of Ganymede, and elsewhere were pictures of the seasons, and of gladiators doing battle in the arena, with cupids acting as secutores. Here we have a glimpse of the social life which the Saxons swept away; but no vestige remains of the cabins of serfs, doubtless clustered around the outer wall that girt this abode of comfort and splendor; for here as elsewhere was the union of patrician wealth and plebeian degradation common to the Roman world.

Of the conversion of the Anglo-Saxons to Christianity the story as told by Baeda in his *Ecclesiastical History* has been too often repeated to require here other than passing allusion. Presently England had her St. George and Ireland her St. Patrick, the former bringing with him a somewhat tarnished reputation for a patron saint; since as Gibbon relates, he had made his fortune at the expense of his honor, swindling the Roman government in an army contract for bacon.

GIBBON

Corrupt as was the church at this early period, giving ready admission to rites and doctrines borrowed from pagan schools and temples, the conversion of Saxon freebooters and colonists to Christianity was doubtless a boon for the people whom they had conquered. It was with this conversion, as Macaulay puts it, that the land which had been lost to view as Britain reappears as England; and in the chronicles of the age there is sufficient evidence that the reign of priestcraft, whatever its evils, was better than the reign of brute violence. We read of the most bloodthirsty of tyrants seized with remorse when at the zenith of their power, laying aside their crowns, devoting their wealth to charitable purposes, and seeking to atone by prayer and penance for the guilt of the past. In times of war the cruelty of the conquerors was mitigated; and in times of peace communication was opened with the great countries of antiquity whose glories had not entirely departed. "Many noble monuments," says Macaulay, "which have since been destroyed or defaced, still retained their pristine magnificence. The dome of Agrippa still glittering with bronze, the mausoleum of Adrian not yet deprived of its columns and statues, the Flavian amphitheatre not yet degraded into a quarry, told to the Mercian and Northumbrian pilgrims some part of the story of that great civilized world which had passed away. The islanders returned with awe deeply impressed on their half opened minds, and told the wondering inhabitants of the hovels of London and York that near the grave of St. Peter a mighty race, now extinct, had piled up buildings which would never be dissolved till the judgment day." Such was the condition of affairs when Alfred the Great appears on the scene, repelling, after a fierce struggle, the last invasions of Danish and other barbarians of the north.

MACAULAY

The youngest of the five sons of King Aethelwulf, Aelfred, or Alfred as he is usually called, was sent when five years of age to Rome, accompanied by a train of wealthy nobles, and as his principal chronicler relates, was anointed king by Leo IV. He was a well-favored lad, gracious of aspect and speech, and though he had little education, except what he gave himself in later years, was almost from his cradle a searcher after wisdom. Like other youths, he cared more for hunting than for books, and in this he was bold and skilful. Within a month after his father's death, which occurred in April, 871, he fought his first battle against the Danes with indecisive results, peace being concluded thereafter. But the Danes returned, and notwithstanding treaties, vows, and as some have it, payments in money, presently drove him from his throne, so that for a time he was glad to take refuge in the forests of Somersetshire. Then comes the story of the cakes, the visit in disguise to the Danish camp, and the final overthrow and expulsion of the invaders, all of which has been a thousand times repeated.

With the wars of Alfred the raids of the Norsemen came for the moment to an end. For centuries these pirate hordes were the scourge of northern Europe, and especially of England, whose shores were but a few leagues distant from their own. They were the most ferocious and vindictive of warriors, hating the very name of Christianity, and inflicting on Christian Saxon even greater atrocities than heathen Saxon inflicted on Christian Kelt. Settling in colonies on the eastern coast, and constantly reënforced from beyond the sea, they gradually spread throughout the fairest portions of the land, draining its wealth, exhausting its resources, and crushing out its nascent civilization. It was a long and terrible struggle, lasting for several generations, each side alternately gaining and losing the supremacy. Defeat was followed by massacre and massacre by retribution; cities were plundered and razed to the ground, and it was not until the eve of the Norman conquest that, through intermarriage and blending of tongues, the two races learned to dwell together in peace. Thus are the English people and the English language an admixture of many elements, having as their base the Keltic, the Saxon, the Scandinavian, and the Norman, but with nearly all the nations of western Europe represented in their component parts.

It was not until the days of Alfred that England possessed a code of laws; for "inter arma silent leges," as the Roman saying is. He was less a lawmaker than a compiler of laws; and that he established trial by jury is one of the many fictions connected with his reign; for this is an institution from time immemorial among the Teutonic races. "I Alfred the king," he says, — to use his own words as rendered in modern English – "gathered together these laws, and had many of them written which our forefathers held — those that I approved. And many of them that I approved not I cast aside by the counsel of my wise men. I dared not write down much of my own; but such as seemed to me the best I have gathered herein, and the rest I have thrown aside." That he founded the university of Oxford is another of the fabrications connected with the name of Alfred, who had he done half of what is ascribed to him, would have surpassed the most glorious achievements of a Caesar or a Charlemagne. Yet on the strength of this story the oldest of Oxford colleges celebrated not many years ago its thousandth anniversary, and it is not improbable that he established at this modern seat of learning a school or academy which in time developed into a college. Certain it is that he had such a school attached to his own residence, and much it was needed; for except the priests, there were probably not a score of persons in England who could understand the ritual or translate a Latin sentence. Himself setting the example, he began the study of Latin at forty years of age, translating the works of Bede, Pope Gregory, and others, and inserting therein treatises of his own, chiefly on politics and religion. Other schools he established in connection with monasteries which he either supported or founded, inviting scholars from foreign lands to aid him in his work. While he cannot be termed the author of English literature, as some would have us believe, it was in his reign that English literature began to be.

OXFORD

Alfred was an excellent business man; a financier as well as a statesman and soldier. His budget, like his code of laws, was the first one framed in England; his revenues he divided into two parts, one for the church, for charity and education, and the other for purposes of government, among which was "the bringing together from all nations, and in numbers almost beyond counting, of workmen skilled in all kinds of building." But perhaps the greatest service which he rendered to his country was the founding of the English navy, without which the land would have been forever subject to the invasions of foreign powers. "And Alfred the King," says his biographer, "commanded that they should make long ships to contend with those of the Danes; twice as long were they, and some had sixty oars and some yet more; swifter they were and steadier and more lofty also. They were neither made after the fashion of the Frisian ships nor after that of the Danes; but as the king judged they would be most useful." Here we have the inception of the most powerful navy in the world; for though there were vessels of war before this time, they were little better than the open boats of the vikings, for which, indeed, they were no match. It was not, however, until several centuries later that England could be termed a maritime power; to the fleets which Sweyn and Canute commanded no effectual resistance was offered, nor is it probable that the one which Harold assembled could have held in check for a single hour the armada of William the Norman.

Of the Normans mention has already been made in connection with the annals of France. Originally a Scandinavian race, and the most dreaded of all the piratical bands which ravaged western Europe, their flotillas were the terror of every coast and their armies penetrated, as I have said, even to the walls of Paris. Settling in one of the most fertile of Gallic provinces, they rapidly acquired the arts of peace, but without losing the qualities which had caused them to be dreaded more than were the destroying hordes of Attila and Genseric. Embracing Christianity, they learned all that the church could teach them; and laying aside their barbarous jargon, they adopted that of the country in which their lot was cast. In a word they became civilized, infinitely more so than were either Saxon or Dane, gradually exercising a powerful influence on the politics and even on the social life of Europe. Their nobles and knights became not only the bravest of soldiers, but the most courtly of gentlemen; and their wealth they expended, not as did the Saxons in gluttony and drunkenness, but on costly mansions, on high-bred steeds and richly decorated armor, while at their banquets, never disgraced by intemperance, were the choicest of meats and wines.

Such was the people which prostrated Saxon England under its feet as completely as Cyrus the elder laid low the might of the Medes. And well perhaps that it was so; for the revolution which for a time wrested from England her freedom ended with giving it new birth, the conquerors gradually changing into countrymen and all that was worth preserving in Saxon institutions being retained in substance if not in form. Yet, for a time, the vanquished races were reduced to a condition of slavery under the name of serfdom, a condition far more degraded than ever was that of the Russian serf. Their lands and all else that they possessed were divided among the invaders; they were liable to enforced labor, and to a penal code most cruelly enforced; in a word, so absolute was their subjection that for more than a century and a half England has no history in the proper sense of the term.

Under the sons and successors of William the Conqueror England first appears as a European power, conquering Normandy as Normandy had conquered England, and later extending her conquests to other portions of France; so that at the accession of the Plantagenets in the person of Henry II, her domain extended southward beyond the channel almost to the border of Spain. But fortunately for both countries, and especially for England, the Plantagenets could not make good their hold on France, though wasting lives by tens of thousands and treasure by hundreds of thousands in the attempt. Had they done so it is doubtful whether the nation would ever have had a separate and independent existence. Her monarchs, her nobles, and her wealthy families would have lived apart from the body of the people, expending their money in luxurious living on the banks of the Seine rather than on the banks of the Thames. Instead of being the language of Shakespeare and Milton, the English tongue would have been a mere dialect, without a literature and

THE THAMES AT RICHMOND

probably without a settled orthography, while riches, fame, and power would have been restricted to those to whom France was the land of their nativity or adoption. Thus the loss of empire south of the channel during the reign of king John was a blessing and not a calamity, as historians would have us believe. Compelled to reside on the sea-girt island which they had subdued, Norman lord and Norman knight gradually made common cause with Saxon thane and earl, for both were alike oppressed with the tyranny of a false and craven monarch. The descendants of those who had fought under the Conqueror, and of those who had fought under Harold, were for the first time drawn together in friendship, with mutual aims and interests, the first fruits of their reconciliation appearing in the Magna Charta, framed for the benefit of both and wrested from the king by their joint exertions. It is at this point that the real history of the English nation begins.

Of the formative period of the British monarchy I have spoken somewhat at length; for this is the period that is least understood, and for which there are few reliable data. As to the later annals of that monarchy it will here suffice to touch only on the most salient features. Among the later Plantagenets and the sovereigns of the houses of Lancaster and York, six out of nine kings were deposed, and five of the six forfeited their lives as well as their crowns; while of the Stuarts one was beheaded, and another driven into exile. This was an age in which physical force was used as a check on misrule, thus bringing the proudest monarch to terms; and it would be difficult for the modern Englishman to realize how rapidly and effectually this check was applied. At the present day the effect of such insurrections and revolutions as have been witnessed in England a score of times would be far more disastrous than the worst form of misgovernment; for with the accumulation of wealth have been undertaken public and private works on a very large scale; so that in case of rebellion, the results of centuries of development and of the outlay of hundreds of millions might perish in a night. The chattel wealth, moreover, — that which is accumulated in warehouses, shops, and dwellings — is many times greater than in the days of the Plantagenets, when wealth consisted mainly in herds and harvests, and when the riches of the entire country in all other forms were less than are now contained in a second or third class city. Manufactures were few and primitive; commercial credit can hardly be said to have existed; and there was no standing army, or none worthy of the name, though an irregular force, or at least an armed mob, could be collected at a moment's notice; for every man was more or less a soldier, if there were few professional soldiers. Nor should we overestimate the evils of these civil wars and disturbances, the farm laborer following his plough and the squire his hounds over the sites of what are now historic battle-fields, within a week after the conflict was ended, and as though it had never occurred.

Between the reign of the Plantagenets and that of the Stuarts, England became wealthy and great, as wealth and greatness were then esteemed. If there was little money in the land, there was an abundance of food and raiment; and as for the memories of "glorious war," there were Cressy, Poitiers, and Agincourt, though followed by no permanent or useful results, except the acquisition of a few million crowns in the way of ransom or indemnity. Of the armada episode I have already spoken in connection with the annals of Spain; and it remains only to be said that this was the first among the notable exploits of the British navy, exploits alternating at times with shameful defeat, as when Van Tromp and De Ruyter swept it from the seas, and the sound of Dutch cannon, heard in London, spread panic fear among its citizens.

From Elizabeth and from certain of her predecessors the nation would tolerate exactions and arbitrary measures which it would not endure at the hands of feebler rulers; and this such stiff-necked monarchs as Charles I and James II soon learned to their cost. After the flight of James and the accession of William III was already established, the polity which embodies in the main the present institutions of England, — a polity which though never strictly defined or observed — was never again permitted to lapse into despotism. The United Kingdom, it may here be said, has no written constitution such as that of the United States; the one which she possesses being the result of prescriptive usages gradually adopted as the fundamental laws of the state. Among these unwritten laws, though implied in the Magna Charta, is that no taxes can be levied except by vote of parliament; nor without that vote could the queen of Great Britain and empress of India collect to-day a sixpence wherewith to pay for her breakfast, albeit her supplies, with those of her numerous offspring and relatives, amounting in all to £600,000 a year, are usually voted as a matter of course and without demur.

But before proceeding further, let us glance for a moment at the condition of England at the close of the reign of Charles II, as described in the graphic pages of Macaulay, a few of whose statements I will quote or in substance repeat; for they are more descriptive and more thoroughly substantiated than any that I could furnish. "Could the England of 1685 be by some magical process set before our eyes, we should not know one landscape in a hundred or one building in ten thousand. The country gentleman would not recognize his own estate; the inhabitant of the town would not recognize his own street, or even his native city. Everything has been changed except the great features of nature and a few massive and durable works of human art. We might find out Snowdon and Windermere, the Cheddar cliffs and Beachy head; we might find out here and there a Norman minster or a castle that witnessed the wars of the Roses; but with

ENGLISH COUNTRY HOUSE

such rare exceptions everything would be strange to us. Many thousands of square miles which are now rich corn land and meadow interspersed with green hedge-rows and dotted with villages and pleasant country seats, would appear as moors overgrown with furze or fens abandoned to wild ducks. We should see straggling huts built of wood and covered with thatch, where we now see manufacturing towns and seaports renowned to the furthest ends of the earth. The capital itself would shrink to dimensions not much exceeding those of its present suburb on the banks of the Thames. No less strange to us would be the garb and manners of the people, the furniture and the equipages, the interior of the shops and dwellings." Such changes in the state of a nation appear at least as well entitled to the notice of an historian as changes of dynasty or ministry.

There were about 5,500,000 people in England and Wales at the death of Charles II; less than one-fifth of the present number, and only a little above the population now contained in the city of London. The growth of the kingdom was by no means uniform; for there were large tracts of country almost in a condition of barbarism long after the opening of the eighteenth century, due to inclement skies and the ravages of war, which do not consist with careful husbandry. Early in the nineteenth century coal was discovered in the northern counties, and proved a more fruitful and permanent source of wealth than any deposits of so-called precious metals, causing the tide of migration to flow northward, and leading to the rapid development of such manufacturing centres as Manchester, Leeds, and Birmingham. Somewhat before this time there was much of lawlessness in the region beyond the Trent. Armed bands of robbers infested the highways; the country seats of the wealthy and even the larger farmhouses were fortified, the inmates sleeping with weapons at their sides and with boiling water in readiness to scald the aggressor who should come within reach. No one thought of visiting these districts without first making his will; judges and barristers travelled on circuit escorted by a strong guard and carrying their provisions, since from one town to another they must journey through a wilderness.

There were not many wealthy men in England in the days of Charles II, — a score or two at most who would now be considered as more than well to do, and even among these the largest incomes seldom exceeded £20,000 a year. The estate of the duke of Ormond yielded £22,000 a year; that of the duke of Buckingham £19,600, and of the duke of Albermale £15,000, with £60,000 in ready money. These were the three richest, or certainly three of the richest of seventeenth century Englishmen, the average revenue of a temporal peer not exceeding £3,000, and of a baronet or member of the house of commons from £800 to £1,000. It was among state officials that the largest incomes were to be found, though they were but temporary, depending on the favor of the monarch or the will of his parliament.

DUKE OF ORMOND

The offices of the first lord of the treasury and of the secretary were each supposed to be worth £100,000 a year; that of the lord lieutenant of Ireland £40,000; and of the lord chancellor an enormous, but unknown amount; while any statesman at the head of some department of affairs could accumulate sufficient to purchase and support a dukedom. Places were for sale and openly for sale, salaries being the smallest part of their gains, while from the premier down to the junior clerk bribery and corruption in their grossest forms were practised without disguise or reproach. Thus did "the merry monarch" pamper his ministers and courtiers, literally gorging them with money while starving his public service; grudging the expense of army and navy, of pensions to aged and needy officers, and of embassies to foreign courts. As Macaulay remarks, "the sumptuous palace to which the populace of London gave the name of Dunkirk house, the stately pavilions, the fish-ponds, the deer park, and the orangery of Euston, the more than Italian luxury of Ham, with its statuary, fountains, and aviaries, were among the many signs which indicated the shortest road to boundless wealth."

Toward the end of the seventeenth century, the total revenue of England did not exceed £1,500,000, and there were £650,000 of debt; toward the end of the nineteenth century the revenue exceeded £90,000,000 and there were £670,000,000 of debt, the latter having risen to as much as £861,000,000 when in 1815 the peace of Paris was ratified; for the wars with America had cost more than £100,000,000, and those with Napoleon more than £300,000,000. Yet in 1685 the public burden was far more grievous to be borne than in 1895, though meanwhile the yearly amount collected in taxes had increased sixty fold, and the amount of the nation's liabilities a thousand fold; for during this period had been developed infinite sources of wealth, and the accumulation of wealth had been on an enormous scale.

In the time of Charles II agricultural products far exceeded in value that of all other fruits of industry; yet only a small portion of the land was cultivated, and that in the rudest fashion. Deer, wild boars, and wild bulls wandered through uncleared forest lands as freely as though they were in the wilds of America. Domestic animals were of inferior quality; horses, for instance, of native breeds being worth on an average not more than fifty shillings apiece. Rotation of crops was little understood, and farming implements and processes were of the most primitive character. For 1696 the total crop of cereals of all descriptions was estimated at less than 10,000,000 quarters, or 80,000,000 bushels, of which only 2,000,000 quarters were in wheat; for wheaten loaves could be afforded only by the wealthy, and the bread set on the tables of farmers and tradesmen would raise a riot in a modern workhouse or prison.

There were some few manufactures, but of insignificant volume, and of manufacturing centres one of the most thriving and populous was Manchester, where perhaps 2,000,000 pounds of cotton a year — a quantity that would not now suffice for a day's consumption — were wrought into fabrics on hand-looms; for Arkwright had not yet taught how to work with the speed and precision of machinery. There was not a single printing-press in this city which now contains hundreds of printing-houses, and which far surpasses in wealth and population such capitals as Berlin and Madrid. Leeds, where to-day is the home of half a million of people, was already boasting of its woollens, and of the immense sales made on its bridge in the open air, — hundreds, nay thousands of pounds on a single market day, greatly to the increase of wealth. Sheffield was proud of its cutlery, and Birmingham of its hardware, though somewhat ashamed, let us hope, of its reputation for the coining of counterfeit money. At these and other centres the owners of workshops and factories grew rich; but the condition of operatives was pitiful in the extreme. Sixpence a day was an average wage for workers at the loom, and this was supplemented by the toil of their children, sometimes not more than seven or eight years of age; so that in the city of Norwich it was stated with an air of exultation that young boys and girls employed in the clothing trade created wealth exceeding by £12,000 a year what was necessary for their support. Money must be made; there were the nobility and gentry, and the innumerable royal progeny to be maintained in idleness. The war of labor against capital had begun, and with a bitter, vehement cry; but as yet there were none to champion its cause, no newspaper even to publish its wrongs. In one of the ballads of the times, now preserved in the British museum, the master clothier is represented as expressing himself as follows:

> *In former ages we used to give,*
> *So that our workfolk like farmers did live;*
> *But the times are changed, we will make them know.*
> *We will make them work hard for sixpence a day,*

Though a shilling they earn if they had their just pay.
If at all they murmur and say 'tis too small,
We bid them choose whether they'll work at all.
And thus do we gain all our wealth and estate,
By many poor men who work early and late.

Among watering places Bath was the most frequented, and already somewhat of a town, since for many centuries it had been the seat of a bishopric, where at times the king held court. Yet it was but a cluster of cottages, cabins, and narrow, filthy streets, enclosed by an ancient Roman wall of which fragments may still be seen. As to the comforts and luxuries offered to visitors who went there in search of health or recreation, a description has been given by one who wrote some three-score years after the revolution which placed William III on the throne. In his younger days, he says, the richest of the patrons who frequented the springs lived in apartments no better than those which were later occupied by their servants. There were no carpets on the floors of dining-rooms; but in their place a coating of soot and small beer, a mixture intended to conceal the dirt. No part of the house was painted, though the chambers set aside for the wealthy and noble were hung with coarse woollen stuffs, and supplied with rush-bottomed chairs; while a slab of freestone for the fireplace, with a poker and pair of tongs, completed the furniture of what was then considered a fashionable lodging. Contrast this with the modern town of Bath, one of the finest of English cities, renowned alike for the elegance of its buildings and the beauty of its site; with spacious streets and terraced slopes in its newer quarters, and in its ancient quarter a fifteenth century abbey church with restorations of recent date.

MATLOCK BATH

And so it is with other cities; not those the products of whose looms and forges are distributed throughout every quarter of the earth, but towns where wealth elsewhere created and accumulated is expended in seeking for health and wholesome recreation. Cheltenham, for instance, is a larger city than any that existed in the time of the Stuarts, London alone excepted. Yet, at the close of the seventeenth century, it is described as a country parish, whose fields, now covered with costly and handsome villas, were well suited for tillage and pasture. About the same date Brighton is mentioned as a place that had once been a prosperous fishing village, with 2,000 people or more, but was then sinking rapidly into decay. The buildings were gradually being swallowed up by the sea, and only a few poor fishermen dried their nets on the cliffs, where rows of neat residences and stately mansions, several miles in length, present their front to the sea.

The metropolis and other cities that require more detailed mention will be reserved for later description. In conclusion let us hear what an eminent writer has to say of the squires and country gentlemen of the seventeenth century, and of the nineteenth; the latter, though described as in the middle of the present cycle, differing but slightly from the types which exist to-day. "The modern country gentleman usually receives a liberal education, passes from a distinguished school to a distinguished college, and has every opportunity to become an excellent scholar. He has generally seen something of foreign countries. A considerable part of his life has been passed as a rule in the capital; and the refinements of the capital follow him into the country. There is perhaps no class of dwellings so pleasing as the rural seats of the English gentry. In the parks and pleasure-grounds, nature, dressed but not disguised by art, wears her most alluring form. In the buildings, good sense and good taste combine to produce a happy union of the beautiful and the graceful. The pictures, the musical instruments, the library would in any other country be considered as proving the owner to be an eminently polished and accomplished man.

ENGLISH COUNTRY HOUSE

"A country gentleman who witnessed the revolution was probably in receipt of about a fourth part of the rent which his acres now yield to posterity. He was therefore, as compared with his posterity, a poor man, and was generally under the necessity of residing, with little interruption, on his estate. To travel on the Continent, to maintain an establishment in London, or even to visit London frequently, were pleasures in which only the richest proprietors could indulge. Many lords of manors had received an education differing little from that of their menial servants. The heir of an estate often passed his boyhood and youth at the family seat, with no better tutors than grooms and gamekeepers, and scarce attained learning enough to sign his name to a document. His chief serious employment was the care of his property. He examined samples of grain, handled pigs, and on market days made bargains over a tankard of ale with drovers and hop merchants. His chief pleasures were commonly derived from field sports, and from an unrefined sensuality. He troubled himself little about decorating his abode, and if he attempted decoration, seldom produced anything but deformity. His table was loaded with coarse plenty, and guests were cordially welcomed to it. The habit of drinking to excess was general in the class to which he belonged, and the ladies of the house, whose business it had been to cook the repast, retired as soon as the dishes had been devoured, and left the gentlemen to their ale and tobacco. The coarse jollity of the afternoon was often prolonged till the revellers were laid under the table."

Such was seventeenth century England, as related in part by Macaulay, whose description, while somewhat highly colored, may be accepted as reliable in the main, though his political narrative is often more eloquent than truthful. It is impossible, for instance, to suppose that James II was such an imbecile and dolt as Macaulay portrays him; nor was William III by any means so capable a monarch, or of such heroic mould as the historian would have us believe. Doubtless the hero of the revolution was a valiant warrior and a competent leader, though his tactics were learned from suffering defeat in the Netherlands at the hands of more able generals. But as a statesman he did not excel, and as a financier he proved himself a failure; the commons for the first time taking upon themselves the control of the revenue, and strictly enforcing their right to appropriate the nation's income to the various branches of expenditure. With all his extravagance, Charles

II had left the country only £665,000 in debt, on which the annual charge was less than £40,000; during the reign of the prince of Orange this debt was increased to £12,767,000, while the war of succession in the days of Queen Anne caused a further increase to £36,175,000.

The reign of Anne is noted chiefly for the wars of Marlborough, the growth of literature, and the South Sea bubble, of which last I have already spoken in connection with the annals of France. As to the wars it need only be said that, however glorious it may have been to lay waste the fairest provinces of France, they resulted in no lasting benefits to England, though with very material benefits to John Churchill, duke of Marlborough, to whom was granted the manor of Woodstock, with a palace erected in its park at a cost of £240,000, besides marriage portions for his daughters, and for the duke and his wife a yearly income of £64,000. While one of the foremost of generals, the victor of Blenheim, in common with the victor of Waterloo, was never a popular man. His vices were serious, and of the character that is most prejudicial to public men. Worst among them were his greed and avarice in accumulating and hoarding money, giving color to the charges of peculation brought against him in his later years. Moreover, he had served two masters, forsaking the cause of James II as soon as it became apparent that the prince of Orange was destined to rule over England. Yet in this respect he was no worse than his associates, all of whom were guilty of similar desertion.

DUKE OF MARLBOROUGH

When the crown of England was offered in 1714 to George Louis, Duke of Cambridge, he was by no means in haste to wear it, tarrying long in Hanover, and when he came, bringing with him his German companions, his German chamberlains and secretaries, and as mistresses, two of the most homely of German fraus, one of whom became the duchess of Kendal and the other the countess of Darlington. They were known to the people, however, as the maypole and the elephant; for the duchess was exceeding lean and tall of stature, and the countess abnormally fat and of unwieldy bulk. Such were the king and court whom English nobles welcomed, while thousands of English citizens cried, Hurrah for King George!

Yet George I was better than the average of monarchs, keeping his compact with his British subjects and ruling with justice and moderation. If he passed most of his time in Hanover, it is not to be wondered at; for his heart was there, and though England was his kingdom, it was never his country; he knew full well that its people had made him their sovereign merely because they wanted him, because he served their turn, sneering at him behind his back, and laughing at his uncouth manners. His reign was brief; for he was more than fifty years of age when appointed to the throne; and death overtook him not in the land that to him was the land of his exile, but in his native country which he loved. He had promised the duchess of Kendal, it is said, to make himself known to her after death; and this he did, as the duchess believed, in the shape of a raven hopping in at the window of her Twickenham villa. Presently the duchess followed him, leaving to her Hanoverian relatives a large amount of cash, jewelry, plate, and other forms of plunder; for if George himself did not steal, he said to his attendants and mistresses, "Take whatever you can get."

In manners the second George was even more outlandish than his father; shaking his fist in the face of his father's courtiers, and calling them rascals, while himself assuming what his father had never assumed, — the right divine of kings to govern wrong — yet he was by no means a despicable nor even an unpopular monarch. His subjects laughed at him because of his eccentricities, which constantly made him appear in a ridiculous light; but nevertheless they liked him; for he was a fairly honest man, certainly more so than his ministers; he was a straightforward, clear-sighted, and above all a brave man; and unto bravery much is forgiven. At Oudenarde he had helped to save the British from disastrous defeat, and at Dettingen the dapper, doughty little king had fought right valiantly. At the latter of these engagements, the last at which a British sovereign appeared in person, his horse ran away with him almost into the enemy's lines; but dismounting, he placed himself at the head of the infantry, shaking his rapier at the French and calling on his men to follow him, in broken English it is true, and lunging like a fencing-master; yet with boldness and spirit.

There is perhaps no period of their history over which the English would sooner draw a veil than the earlier portion of the reign of George II. Walpole, called into office after the widespread ruin which attended the collapse of the South Sea bubble, still remained in power. He was an excellent business man, at a time when the house of commons contained few men of business; he was possessed of strong sagacity and foresight, and so far he was well fitted to shape the destinies of a nation whose wants were material rather than political. But he was himself one of the most corrupt and mercenary of all the members of a corrupt and venal parliament, at a time when votes were bought at election day and sold in the commons for pensions, place, or cash. Yet let us not judge him too harshly; for this system did not originate with him, nor under him did it reach its height, his successor, Henry Pelham, using the arts of bribery and dissimulation in such fashion as even Walpole himself would have been ashamed to adopt. Meanwhile England was prosperous, and Englishmen were living in peace and plenty in their bluff, independent way.

Let us hear what Thackeray has to say as to the administration and character of this famous or infamous premier, who combined, in truth, a strange admixture of qualities. "But for his resolute counsels and good-humored resistance, we might have had German despots attempting a Hanoverian regimen over us; we should have had revolt, commotion, want, and tyrannous misrule in place of a quarter of a century of peace, freedom, and material prosperity, such as the country never enjoyed until that corrupter of parliaments, that dissolute, tipsy cynic, that courageous lover of peace and liberty, that great citizen, patriot, and statesman governed it. In religion he was little better than a heathen; cracked ribald jokes at bigwigs and bishops, and laughed at high church and low. In private life the old pagan revelled in the lowest pleasures; he passed his Sundays tippling at Richmond, and his holidays bawling after dogs, or boozing at Houghton with boors over beef and punch. He cared for letters no more than his master did; he judged human nature so meanly that one is ashamed to have to own that he was right, and that men could be corrupted by means so base. But, with his hireling house of commons, he defended liberty for us; with his incredulity lie kept churchcraft down. There were parsons at Oxford as double-dealing and dangerous as any priests out of Rome, and he routed them both. He gave Englishmen no conquests; but he gave them peace and ease and freedom; the three per cents nearly at par, and wheat at five or six and twenty shillings a quarter."

It was during the reigns of Anne and the two Georges that literature and the influence of the press first made themselves felt as powers in the land; for though the literature of the Elizabethan era may have been more resplendent, it brought neither honors nor wealth to authors, none of whom, except perhaps Spenser and Shakespeare, could live comfortably on the proceeds of the pen. But at the later period of which I speak, there were not a few whose toil was fairly rewarded. Pope, for instance, accumulated what was then a fortune; Dryden, Addison, and others earned at least a moderate income, and before the death of George II, in 1770, Johnson was in possession of a competence. In the time of Walpole, though himself indifferent to literature of whatever kind, large sums of money and valuable patronage were bestowed on those who could write ably in support of the government. Newspapers and other periodicals, of which, until the close of the seventeenth century there were none outside of London, began to multiply apace and to be widely distributed. Yet thousands of newspapers and hundreds of books are printed to-day for one that was published in the days of the Georges; while it is probable that such writers as Walter Besant and William Black receive more for the work of a single year than the founders of *The Spectator* or the first of English lexicographers received in a lifetime.

While in culture and wealth the people had steadily progressed, their habits, and especially their drinking habits, had not changed much for the better since the era before describes. Long before that time this vice was all too common among Englishmen, as even today it is; though to get drunk every night is no longer considered as among the indispensable accomplishments of a gentleman. "Superfluity of drink," remarks Tom Nash, writing in the days of Elizabeth, '"is a sin that is accounted honorable." Elizabeth herself drank deeply at breakfast from a foaming tankard of ale. "In England," says Iago, "they are most potent in potting. Your Dane, your German, and your swag-bellied Hollander are nothing to the English." In the reign of Anne hard drinking was fashionable, and many of the foremost men of the day were also the foremost of tipplers. Addison was not free from this common failing of his times. The earl of Oxford, whose character was otherwise beyond reproach, often came drunk into the presence of the queen. Bolingbroke, even when in office, would pass the entire night over his cups, and then, after binding a wet napkin round his head to drive away the effect, set forth without sleep to conduct the affairs of the nation. Of Walpole it is related by Lecky that, when a young man, his father would pour into his glass a double portion of wine, saying, "Come, Robert, you shall drink twice while I drink once; for will not permit the son in his sober senses to be witness to the intoxication of his father." Such training bore its fruit. Even among women intemperance was not uncommon. Describing the parties held at Tunbridge Wells, where music was the entertainment and tea the usual refreshment, Gay speaks of a certain damsel who was somewhat eccentric in her tastes. "I have known," he says, "some young ladies who, if ever they prayed, would ask for some equipage or title, or perhaps for a husband; but this lady, who is but seventeen and has £30,000 to her fortune, places all her wishes on a pot of good ale." Among the lower classes matters were even worse; for nearly all their money was expended in drink, and for this they were content to go without sufficient food or decent clothing. In 1736 there were more than 7,000 licensed dram-shops in London, one to every six houses and to every 40 inhabitants, to say nothing of 3,200 beer-shops where gin was sold in secret; while in the provinces, signs displayed on road-side taverns informed the wayfarer that he could get well drunk for a penny, dead drunk for twopence, and without further expense sleep off the effects of his orgies on the clean straw that lay in the cellar.

Gambling was also a fashionable vice, especially during the fever of speculation which infected all classes at the time of the South Sea mania. "Gaming," writes Seymour, "has become so much the fashion, that he who in company should be ignorant of the games in vogue would be reckoned low-bred and hardly fit for conversation." "Books! Prithee," exclaimed the dowager duchess of Marlborough, "don't talk to me about books; the only books I want to know are men and cards." Every one played at cards and played for money, from royalty down to the clergy, a portion of the stakes being sometimes devoted to charity. Says a chronicler of the time of George II, "This being Twelfth-day, their majesties the prince of Wales, and the three eldest princesses went to the chapel royal, preceded by the heralds. The duke of Manchester carried the sword of state. The king and prince made offering at the altar of gold, frankincense, and myrrh, according to the annual custom. At night their majesties played at hazard with the nobility for the benefit of the groom-porter, and 'twas said the king won 600 guineas, the queen 360, the duke of Grafton and the earl of Portmore several thousands."

In London there were several gambling resorts, chief among which was White's chocolate-house, where the duke of Devonshire lost a valuable estate at a game of basset. In the green-rooms of theatres thousands of pounds changed hands in a single night. Many fashionable women were inveterate gamesters, one of the most notorious being the daughter of the premier, Henry Pelham, while in her *Diary* Lady Cowper mentions sittings of the court at which the lowest stake was 200 guineas. Lotteries were also in vogue, and were used by the ministry in power as a means of raising money without loss of popularity. In 1711 Addison writes to a friend in Ireland, "I cannot forbear telling you that last week I drew a prize of £1,000 in the lottery." Westminster bridge, begun in 1736, was mainly built from the proceeds of lotteries; and thus were acquired by the government the famous Harleian manuscripts and the library and collection of Sir Hans Sloan, deposited in Montague house; such was the origin of the British museum.

Let us turn for a moment to the brighter side of English society; and this I cannot describe better than in the words of Thackeray, though tinged a little with fustian and flattery, and referring to a somewhat later period. "It is to the middle class we must look for the safety of England; the working educated men, the good clergy not corrupted into parasites by hopes of preferment, the tradesmen rising into manly opulence, the painters pursuing their gentle calling, the men of letters in their quiet studies; these are the men we love and like to read of in the last age. How small the grandees and the men of pleasure look beside them! How contemptible the story of the George III court squabbles are beside the recorded talk of dear old Johnson. What is the grandest entertainment at Windsor compared to a night at the club over its modest cups, with Percy and Langton and Goldsmith, and poor Bozzy at the table. I declare I think of all the polite men of that age Joshua Reynolds was the finest gentleman. And they were good, as well as witty and wise, those dear old friends of the past. Their minds were not debauched by excess, or effeminate with luxury. They toiled their noble day's labor; they rested and took their kindly pleasure; they cheered their holiday meetings with generous wit and hearty interchange of thought;

they were no prudes, but no blush need follow their conversation; they were merry, but no riot came out of their cups. Ah! I would have liked a night at the Turk's head, even though bad news had arrived from the colonies, and Doctor Johnson was growling at the rebels; to have sat with him and Goldy, and to have heard Burke, the finest talker in the world, and to have had Garrick flashing in with a story from his theatre. I like, I say, to think of that society, and not only how pleasant and how wise, but how good they were."

At this time there were many thousands of middle-class families in easy circumstances, both in the metropolis and in the provinces; families, that is, with incomes of from £300 to £500 a year, equal in purchasing power to five times that amount to-day. Besant in his *London* gives the expenses of a well-to-do householder in 1760 at about £400 a year, against £1,300 in 1850, while in 1900 they would probably not be far short of £2,000. The household is supposed to consist of husband and wife, four children, and two servant maids, the scale of living being the same in both instances. For rent and taxes £66 are allowed in 1760 and £150 in 1850; for the table and for fuel £190 and £420; for clothing £64 and £120, and for education £8 and £143 respectively. In 1760 nothing is allowed for travelling or for books or other literature, while in 1850, £190 is devoted to these purposes; while the items of £11 and £42 set aside for sickness indicates almost a fourfold increase in doctors' bills. Habits were far more simple then than now, and except for drinking, far more healthful, especially as to diet and exercise. In the morning tea or chocolate was served with a light and early breakfast, and dinner was at two, when the business of the day was finished or left to subordinates. There were certain dishes for certain days, as roast goose at Michaelmas, salt beef at Martinmas, roast beef with beans and butter at Midsummer, and on Easter day, veal with a gammon of bacon and a tansy pudding; while at dessert there were always sweetmeats and fruits, and to drink — madeira and port.

Everyone had his club, usually in a tavern or coffee-house, where he transacted business in the morning and chatted and tippled in the evening. It was at these clubs that the commerce of London was largely conducted, and there was one or more for every class, chief among which were Garraway's, Johnathan's, and Lloyd's, while the Jamaica was for those engaged in the West Indian trade, the Baltic for those who dealt with Russia, and for booksellers there was the Chapter in Paternoster row. Women lived much apart, visiting among themselves in the day time and in the evening remaining at home; for the streets were infested with thieves and footpads, so that no woman ventured abroad after dark without escort. Their chief occupations were needlework, painting, the copying of music, and the confection of cakes and pastry; among their recreations was an occasional visit to Vauxhall, where they enjoyed at will the music and singing, the supper, and the glass of hot punch that followed.

The blessings of a headless monarchy appear at this juncture. It was a fortunate thing for England that the first of the Georges were dull-witted, unambitious rulers, spending much of their time in Hanover, keeping out of the way, and leaving their kingdom to take care of itself. Thus troubles were avoided; for sovereign and subject perfectly understood each other, the former being rather the servant than the monarch of the people over whom he ruled in name; but always well treated, well tipped, and with perfect liberty to come and go where and whensoever he pleased. With George III, however, it was different; he was a native of the country, proud of his nativity, and proposed to reign as a king and not as a puppet, though no more fitted to govern England than his predecessors, who never attempted to govern. Doubtless he did his best, this dull, obstinate, bigoted man, when he ascended the throne on which he should never have sat during this period that witnessed so many stirring events, — the decapitation or banishment of kings, the Napoleonic episode, and the loss of the American colonies, "the brightest jewel in the British crown." He lived according to his lights; he practised all the virtues that he knew, and he acquired all the knowledge that his slender wits would permit. "His household," says Thackeray, "was a model of a country gentleman's household. It was early; it was kindly; it was charitable; it was frugal; it was orderly; it must have been stupid to a degree which we shudder now to contemplate."

Had the throne of England been occupied by an abler monarch than George III; had an abler minister than North been at the head of the nation's affairs, it is by no means impossible, or even improbable that the United States would have been to-day one of the fairest portions of the British empire; or if they had separated, it would have been on friendly terms, and without shedding a drop of blood. But as resistance grew stronger in the colonies, so did the stubborn king become more determined that they must be forced into submission; and in this he had on his side the prejudices, but never the intelligence of the community. Presently Burgoyne trips forth from his London club on St. James's street to conquer America, returning somewhat crestfallen after his defeat. Cornwallis, though at first victorious, fares no better in the end; for with the aid of a French fleet and a disciplined army under Lafayette, Washington makes short work of the British. Thus was confirmed the prophecy which Chatham uttered in the hall of Westminster; "You cannot, my lords, you cannot conquer America!" And not only were the colonies free; but England as a nation was glad that they were free.

LORD NORTH

In the reign of the fourth George, and of the fourth William, there is nothing that need here detain us; nor need we dwell on the events of Victoria's reign, which are doubtless familiar to the reader. Her long administration of well-nigh threescore years, longer than that of any former sovereign, has been in the main one of the most prosperous eras in the nation's annals, though chequered by such episodes, as the Indian mutiny, the Crimean war, and the ceaseless pettifogging wars in which England appears to delight. Seldom has been witnessed more able statesmanship than that of Sir Robert Peel, of Earl Russell, of Gladstone and Disraeli; Gladstone's financial measures especially tending toward increase of wealth, though of late the country has not been overburdened with prosperity. As to the queen herself, she has done all that the nation expected of her, all that her immediate predecessors have done, and all that her successors can do; that is to say she has done nothing. Though nominally holding the power of veto, it is never exercised; and except holding court, which could well be dispensed with, and affixing an occasional signature to acts of parliament, and to public documents, it would be difficult to define the functions of royalty as it exists in England to-day.

GLADSTONE

It is a somewhat expensive operation, this signing of documents and keeping of court, from which the better class of British nobility holds aloof. First there are voted by parliament what are termed the queen's supplies, — £325,000 a year for her household expenses and £60,000 for her privy purse. The portion of the prince of Wales is £40,000; of his wife £10,000, and of their children £60,000; to the dukes of Edinburgh and Connaught are granted £25 000 each; to the princesses Christian, Louise, Beatrice, and to the duchess of Albany, each £6,000; and to the empress Friedrich of Prussia £8,000, all these being children of the queen. Then there are her cousins; of whom the duke of Cambridge receives £12,000; the duchess of Teck £5,000, and the duchess of Mecklenburg-Strelitz £3,000; other pensions amounting to £25,000, or nearly £600,000 in all, for maintaining the pageant of royalty. But even with this the royal family is not content, and seldom is a session of parliament held at which one or more of its members do not apply for an additional sum. During the session of 1896, for example, a further allowance of £1,800 a year was demanded for the duke of Cambridge, giving rise to much comment and discussion, as well indeed it might; for it was pitiful to see this aged and royal mendicant, whose fortune is far in the millions, attempting to smuggle a bill through the commons for a retiring pension as ex-commander-in-chief of the British army.

Against Queen Victoria, neither subjects nor foreigners have a word to say, whether as a queen or as a woman; for she has done the best that she could; but the days of monarchy are numbered, and the world is becoming tired of supporting royalty and royal families of sickly boys and silly girls, albeit the reigning family of England does not belong to this category. Yet in that country sovereignty, prerogative, and church have long since given way to civil rights, to civil and religious freedom. While old-fashioned toryism is not entirely extinct, among the people at large, king worship and queen worship are as much among the things of the past as are the pillory and the mutilation of political offenders. Partly as a consequence of this freedom, and also as the result of better morals and manners, servility to rulers is out of date; and though servile forms and ceremonies may still exist, no longer do men cringe and women compete for favor in a court where woman's shame was not accounted as dishonor.

If not yet ripe for self-government, there are several European nations which would appear to be on the eve of such a change; and none more so than Great Britain, where at times revolution seems imminent, and when it comes, will probably come as quietly as at the deposition or rather the flight of James II, without bloodshed or clash of arms. That it has not come sooner is due to the fact that there is little to be gained by it; for the yoke of royalty sits so lightly on the people that its touch is barely felt, and the change from monarchy to republicanism would be rather one of forms than of institutions. But in Europe there is much to be gained, as is shown in the wonderful prosperity of France, notwithstanding the payment of an enormous war indemnity and the loss of hundreds of millions sunk in the Panama canal. Here perhaps may now be living, as yet unknown to fame, another Napoleon, who making war on monarchs, not for ambition but for his country's sake, and in the name of human freedom, may cause Europe again to resound with the crash of continental thrones. When the news of Napoleon's death reached England, it chanced that Hazlitt and Charles Lamb were conversing about the great general "whom both of us liked," says Hazlitt, "but for entirely different reasons; he for putting down the rabble of the people, and I for putting down the rabble of the kings."

Of ancient London and of the annals of London much that is of interest might here be said; but this I must pass over as briefly as possible; for it is rather with the modern city that we are now concerned. Long before the first of the Caesars set foot in Britain, a collection of huts in the midst of marsh or forest occupied the site of what is now the commercial metropolis of the world. In the time of Nero it had already become a considerable mart of traffic, visited by merchants from many lands, though never regarded as the capital of Roman Britain. There was a wall around it, and there were several gates, among them those afterward known as Ludgate, Billingsgate, Aldgate, Bishopsgate, Newgate, and others. At a somewhat later period it was a mile in length by half a mile in breadth, and at the close of the Roman occupation was the abode of culture and wealth.

LUDGATE CIRCUS

With the departure of the legions quickly disappeared all traces of Roman civilization; and says a chronicler of the age in his narrative recently published for the first time: "Where now was the wealth of this famous province? It was gone. Where was the trade of Augusta?" — the fifth century name for London. "That, too, was gone. Nothing was brought for export; the roads were closed; the river was closed; there was nothing in fact to send; nay there were no more households to buy the things we formerly sent them. They lived now by the shore and in the recesses of the forest, who once lived in great villas, lay on silken pillows, and drank the wine of Gaul and Spain." Yet a remnant was left, a remnant of the baser sort who, crawling out of the dens where they crouched in abject fear of Saxon free-booters, and finding no enemy in sight, bethought themselves that the entire city was theirs to plunder at will. Then they collected all the valuables which the people had been compelled to leave behind them, — "the sacred vessels from the churches and the rich embroidered robes of silk worn by the priests. They found soft stuffs in the villas with which they wrapped themselves; they found curtains, rich hangings, pillows, cushions, carpets — all of which they took. The carved work and statues, books, pictures, and things which they understood not they broke in pieces or burned."

About half a century later, it chanced that a band of east Saxons, in search of a suitable place for settlement, came in sight of the city, and though looking rather for a spot where they could grow their crops and keep their cattle, determined to capture it. As the gates were closed, they blew their horns and summoned the inhabitants to surrender. But no answer was returned; neither was arrow, stone, or other missile discharged at the invaders. Then, battering in one of the gates, they entered, shouting their war-cry and brandishing their weapons. But soon they ceased to shout; for there were none to oppose them, and they found themselves in a deserted city. Surrounded with spacious gardens overgrown with weeds were the walls of what had once been handsome villas, then crumbling into decay; they were roofless; the tessellated pavements of court-yards were broken into fragments, and the fountains choked with rubbish, while grass grew in streets where still the deep ruts worn by wagon wheels showed signs of traffic. Passing onward to the river side, the Saxons found there a few thatched huts, in the midst of which fires were burning, and on the fires fish were frying in pans. The people had taken to flight when they heard the Saxon war-cry, and gathering such of their effects as they could carry, took refuge in the trackless forest which lay toward the north, where no enemy could follow.

Thus lay the city of London a city of the dead; but not for long; since the tide of war rolled westward, and pirate craft no longer hovered around the broad reaches of the Thames. The country was at peace; and presently a few traders ventured up the river, entering the port of which little but its memory remained. Thence they sent out men who displayed to the nearest settlers swords and spearheads, all of the finest workmanship, and offered in barter for hides and wool. These were probably the first commercial travellers; certainly the first of which any record has survived. With the revival of trade, the city began to revive; for there were many who preferred to live there rather than spend the long days toiling all alone on their farms, some, more nimble-witted than the rest, perceiving how they could live and accumulate wealth, not by their own labor but by exchanging the products of others' labor; that is to say by commerce. Then came more merchants and more workmen, the one class keeping the other poor; else there were no chance for the few to get rich. Such was the origin of modern London, which, when the first of its bishops took charge of his diocese at the opening of the seventh century, had again become a lively mart of trade, its quays well lined with shipping and its streets astir with traffic.

Toward the fortification and embellishment of London the Saxons did little, but the Normans contributed much; beginning with the Tower, originally built to overawe disaffected citizens, of whom there were not a few among its 40,000 inhabitants in the days of William the Conqueror. In the thirteenth and fourteenth centuries occurred many destructive fires, famines, and pestilences, costing the lives of thousands, while the rebellion of Wat Tyler and the outbreak of which Jack Cade was the leader were accompanied with burning and pillaging. In the time of Elizabeth the prosperity, as well as the patriotism of the people, was shown by liberal contributions in money, men and ships to resist the attack of the armada. In this, the golden age of England as some have termed it, the increase of trade was beyond all precedent; and especially in the capital, whose merchants the queen treated well; so that during her reign the commercial metropolis of the world was transferred from the city on the Scheldt to the city on the Thames. This, however, was due rather to the able management of Thomas Gresham, who as royal agent at Antwerp, was not slow to turn to the advantage of London the heavy losses incurred by Antwerp through the wars of the Netherlands. He it was who built the Royal exchange and the college which bears his name, who took charge of the queen's finances and negotiated her loans, while scores of trading associations were founded about this period, of which only the Hudson's Bay company now exists.

Gresham had every advantage that birth, wealth, and education could bestow, beginning life as his uncle's apprentice, then being appointed a member of the Mercer's company, and after sojourning in the Low Countries, opening a shop on Lombard street, in front of which was his family crest. In it were for sale gold and silver plate, chains, rings, jewelry, and lace, with coins both ancient and modern. He also conducted a banking business, loaning money at ten to twelve per cent, then the current rate, purchasing bullion, and issuing letters of credit. His career was paralleled somewhat by that of Whittington; for both acted as the financial agents of the reigning sovereign, whose favor they enjoyed; both were mere mercers and merchant adventurers, and both kept shops of which they had too much good sense to be ashamed.

In 1664 began the great plague of London, which cost the lives of 100,000 people, and doubtless would have cost many more but for the fire which came two years later to purge and purify. Yet it was a somewhat expensive blessing, the destruction of property being estimated at £10,000,000, the greatest on record up to that time since the burning of Rome in the days of Nero. The buildings swept out of existence covered an area a mile and a half in length by a mile in width, and included 132,000 dwellings, 89 parish churches, and many public edifices, among which were St. Paul's cathedral and the Royal exchange. In the reign of Queen Anne, when the capital first began to assume its modern aspect, the storm of 1703 caused damage to the amount of £2,000,000, overthrowing or unroofing houses and driving vessels on the river shore. Finally there were the "no-popery" riots of 1780, when the mansions of the wealthy were plundered or burned, and nearly forty conflagrations were counted at one time in various districts.

Notwithstanding these disasters, the metropolis continued to grow and to prosper, many of the finest streets and structures dating from the latter half of the eighteenth century, to which period belong the bank of England, Somerset house, the Mansion house, and the Horse-guards. In the nineteenth century were erected Buckingham palace, the houses of parliament, the new courts of law, London and Waterloo bridges, the British museum, the National gallery, the mint, the post-office, the customhouse, with all the vast array of costly mansions and business blocks now included in Belgravia and the West end. In a word, both municipality and citizens have of late been constructing spacious thoroughfares and handsome buildings as if this were their sole object and occupation in life.

HORSE GUARDS

The present city of London occupies portions of four different counties, the northern section lying in Middlesex and Essex, and the southern and less important section, on the opposite side of the Thames, in Surrey and Kent. The city proper, though a county in itself, is of comparatively small extent, and built, as is much of the outer city, with little regard to plan, the streets, except those of recent construction, running in confused and intricate lines, faulty in connection and with insufficient means of communication, greatly to the impediment of traffic. Thus the finest architectural effects are marred through overcrowding, while some of the thoroughfares leading to the West end are narrow, crooked, and shabby, the Strand, so named from skirting the river bank, now covered with buildings, being one of the busiest and broadest arteries of trade. About midway in the Strand, and adjacent to the new courts of justice completed in 1882 at a cost of £2,200,000, stood Temple bar, built in 1670 by Christopher Wren, and removed in 1878 as an obstruction which could be no longer tolerated. Regent street is the widest and most fashionable of London's public ways, the splendor of its shops offsetting the plainness and monotony of its architecture. It leads into Piccadilly, the eastern portion of which is filled with shops and the western with clubs and mansions, in no way remarkable as buildings unless it be for incongruity of design. Yet this is a pleasant quarter, fronting on a spacious roadway and overlooking Green park and Trafalgar square, the latter with its fountains and statuary above which towers the Nelson column. Near by and parallel with it is Pall Mall, so named from the game of pail mail — in Italian palla a ball and malleo a mallet — introduced into England in the days of Charles I as the prototype of croquet. Here is in truth a street of modern palaces, mainly of Grecian or Italian style, for this is the very centre of club and hotel life, though late in the seventeenth century merely a suburban promenade. Close at hand is Waterloo place, with its Crimean and other monuments; and in this neighborhood is the Haymarket, now of unsavory fame, but noted for its historic temple of the drama, and as the spot where Addison wrote for the few shillings a week that kept him from starvation. In the shops of Oxford street, of which Tottenham Court and Charing Cross roads are continuations, is transacted an enormous volume of business, and here are many buildings of modern and tasteful pattern.

TRAFALGAR SQUARE

Such are a few of the more prominent thoroughfares in the heart of the West end; but as London streets are 3,000 miles in length, and nearly 8,000 in number, they cannot here be described in detail. More than 5,000,000 persons dwell in this huge metropolis, and there are 600,000 buildings, of which about 1,500 are churches and 7,800 are public houses, or saloons as they are termed in America. The annual increase of population is estimated at 70,000, or more than sufficient to people a city, as also is the pauper class, at least 110,000 in number. Of the industrial and commercial classes there are probably not far from 1,000,000; of domestic servants 350,000; and of the unoccupied, or those whose occupations cannot be classified, 1,500,000; for a large percentage of the men and perhaps one-half of the women belong to this category, either from choice or necessity.

OXFORD STREET

Notwithstanding the enormous space covered by suburban villas and cottages, each year a new city is being added to that which already covers an area of 125 square miles. In the fashionable quarters the dwellings are not remarkable for taste or beauty of design; and close to some of them are the squalid thoroughfares tenanted by the working classes, though for the most part these are housed in the dreary and densely peopled districts east of the city proper. Parks and public squares are plentiful, those in the West end alone extending over 900 acres, almost in the heart of the capital, and adjacent to each other. The oldest is St. James's park, laid out as a pleasure ground by Charles II, and rearranged in the present century with skilful blending of water and foliage. In Green park are rows of shade trees, and at the point where it borders on Piccadilly are flower-beds carefully tended, imparting to this neighborhood a bright and cheerful aspect. Hyde Park, the largest of the group, was originally a portion of the manor of Hyde, and belonged to the estates pertaining to Westminster abbey. On the abolition of monasteries and the seizure of their property by Henry VIII it passed into possession of the crown, and in 1652, though of much larger size than the present enclosure, was sold for about £17,000. Repurchased soon afterward for public use, it soon became, as to-day it is, the favorite out-door resort of beauty and fashion, and also of loungers of all nationalities and conditions. Among its attractions are fine expanses of lawn interspersed with shrubbery, parterres of flowers, and the most stately of English oaks, while at the ornamental lake known as the Serpentine, bathing in summer and skating in winter are permitted at certain hours. During what is known as the London season, its spacious avenues are crowded with handsome and costly equipages, one known as Rotten row being set apart for equestrians. Of its nine principal gateways, the one known as Hyde Park corner, its arches adorned with reliefs in imitation of the Elgin marbles, was constructed in 1828 at a cost of £17,000; while on the Marble arch in front of Buckingham palace was expended £80,000. Completing the chain of the larger West end pleasure-grounds are Kensington gardens, with their avenues of rare plants, shrubbery, and flowering trees, adjacent to which is Kensington palace, the birthplace of Queen Victoria, but though formerly a royal residence containing little worthy of note. Elsewhere are many open spaces, chief among which are Regent park in the northwestern section of the city, and Greenwich park in the suburb of that name.

MARBLE ARCH, HYDE PARK

KENSINGTON GARDENS

The greater part of London, so far as contained in the city limits, has been virtually rebuilt within the last century, and its streets much altered and improved, the Metropolitan board now possessing a certain control as to the construction of new thoroughfares. The board is by no means sparing of expense, having paid for the building, widening, and other improvements of streets, within the last thirty years, more than £10,000,000, of which a large proportion has been returned through sales of property. Then there is the Thames embankment, with its wall of granite blocks supporting a beautiful thoroughfare and promenade. Its cost exceeded £3,000,000, the portion known as the Victoria embankment, between Westminster and Blackfriars bridge, including 37 acres of reclaimed land, used in part as ornamental grounds. In the Albert embankment, on the southern side of the river, are about nine acres, mainly occupied by the buildings of St. Thomas' hospital, costing £500,000, with an annual revenue of £40,000, and treating nearly 100,000 patients a year.

Of the twelve bridges which span the Thames, apart from railroad structures, the most easterly is the Tower bridge of steel and stone, opened in 1894 at a cost of more than £1,000,000. Including the approaches, it is half a mile in length, with a carriage way 30 feet and a foot-way 140 feet above the high water level of the river, the central span being furnished with drawbridges for the passage of tall-masted vessels. Not far from it is London bridge; and at this point begins the great line of shipping extending along miles of wharves and quays, yet so closely packed that we might almost step from one craft to another. London bridge, though not as now it stands, is the oldest, and until 1769 was the only bridge in the metropolis. The ancient structure was completed nearly seven centuries ago, in the reign of King John, and upon it were erected rows of houses on either side, with a chapel dedicated to St. Thomas of Canterbury. The present bridge, 930 feet long and 54 in width, supported on five granite arches, and with lamp-posts made from the cannon captured in the Peninsular war, was finished in 1831 after an outlay of nearly £2,000,000. Yet it is now entirely insufficient for the requirements of a traffic which centres largely at this point, more than 17,000 vehicles and 120,000 pedestrians crossing it daily; so that in the busiest hours it is almost impassable. Blackfriars, the second bridge, was rebuilt for £320,000 in 1869, with iron arches resting on a granite foundation; and for Southwark bridge, also with iron arches and stone piers, the expense was £800,000. Westminster bridge is a fine composition, and among others are Waterloo, Lambeth, Vauxhall, and Charing Cross suspension bridges, the total cost of London bridges probably exceeding £9,000,000. There are also street bridges, as the one over Farringdon road, supported by iron columns, and on the parapet bronze statues of science, art, commerce, and agriculture. In this connection may be mentioned the Thames tunnel, on the construction of which were expended £450,000 and eighteen years of work. Opened for traffic in 1843, it was afterward purchased by the Great Eastern railway company. Several tunnels are in contemplation in Europe and America.

LONDON BRIDGE

Close to the Tower bridge, and a little to the east of the ancient city walls, is the most interesting spot in England from an historic point of view; and that is the Tower of London. Founded, as I have said, by William the Conqueror, it was originally a royal palace as well as a stronghold, though better known to fame as the prison whence many a political offender was taken forth to execution on the neighboring Tower hill. Its present use is mainly as an arsenal, though still kept in repair as a fortress; while in different parts of the building are stationed the yeomen of the guard, or beef-eaters as they are commonly termed, this being a corruption of the French buffetiers, or attendants at the buffet. There are four principal entrances; the Water gate, the Traitors' gate, the Iron gate, and the Lions' gate, the last so called because here a menagerie was formerly kept for the delectation of royalty. The white tower, or keep, is the most ancient portion, and this it was that William of Normandy built on a site before occupied by the fortifications erected by Alfred the Great. In the inner ward are a dozen towers, at one time serving as prisons; as the bell tower, where Queen Elizabeth when a princess was confined by her sister Mary; and the bloody tower, where, as is said, the sons of Edward IV were murdered by assassins in the pay of Richard III.

BELL TOWER PRISON

In the council chamber, the banqueting hall, and other apartments is a collection of old armor dating from the time of the ancient Britons, and including the weapons of many nations and periods, Greek, Roman, Etruscan, Persian, Japanese, and African, though with special relation to England and her wars. In a series of equestrian and other figures is shown the war panoply of British warriors from the days of Edward I to the time of James II. There is the richly damascened armor worn by Henry VIII and the costly suit which the emperor Maximilian of Germany presented to him on the eve of his marriage with Catharine of Arragon, the badges of Henry and his elderly spouse appearing frequently among the many ornaments inlaid with gold and silver. Queen Elizabeth is here, on bold charger mounted, and ready to do battle with the Spaniard. There is the suit worn by Charles I, and that which Henry, Prince of Wales, wore in 1612, heavily inlaid with gold; while among the most valuable contributions from foreign lands are a spear-head unearthed from the plain of Marathon, and a full suit of ancient Greek armor found in a tomb at Cumae.

But to the average visitor the most interesting chambers are those in Wakefield tower, where is the repository of the crown jewels and regalia valued at £3,000,000. First may be mentioned St. Edward's crown, the original of which, with other insignia of royalty, was sold after the execution of Charles I and replaced after the restoration, though still retaining its ancient name, the new crown being first used at the coronation of Charles II. The crown made for Queen Vctoria in 1838 is one of the finest specimens of the goldsmith's art, containing nearly 2,800 diamonds, and in front an uncut ruby, presented, as is said, by a Castilian noble to the Black Prince, and glistening on the helmet of Henry V at the battle of Agincourt. The crown which Prince Albert wore is of gold set with jewels, and that of the prince of Wales is of pure gold. The Royal sceptre and the sceptre fashioned for Victoria are richly begemmed and bejewelled, as is the golden circlet set with brilliant and pearls, worn by the wife of James II. There are also royal bracelets, royal spurs, and royal vessels of various kinds, as the gold basin from which the queen's alms are distributed on

Maundy Thursdays, the silver baptismal font of her children, and the silver wine fountain presented to Charles II by the corporation of Plymouth.

CROWN JEWELS

From the comparative solitude of Tower hill one may pass in a few minutes into the roar of traffic in Cheapside, where vehicles and pedestrians are so densely wedged together that hardly a glimpse of street or sidewalk can be had in business hours. It is lined with gaudy shops, and near by some yet more sombre repositories of wealth, yet all attractive, at least as to their contents; for here, almost from time immemorial, have been the headquarters of London jewellers and mercers. From its western end a lane in rear of the general post-office leads to Goldsmith's hall, where are many curiosities and portraits of former celebrities; for the Goldsmiths' company was incorporated in 1327, since which time it has been the chief authority in everything pertaining to the craft, and still puts its stamp on most of the gold and silver ware of English manufacture.

But on our way we have passed the wealthiest and most influential of all British institutions; and here we must linger a moment, for this is no other than the bank of England, "the old lady of Threadneedle street" as it is affectionately or sometimes derisively termed. Though enclosing a space of nearly four acres, the external walls are windowless; the building, which is of the plainest, being lighted from interior courts for the better security of its contents. For nearly a century and a half after it was founded, in 1694, by the Scotch financier William Paterson, it was the only joint-stock bank in the metropolis; the London and Westminster being the next, soon followed by a score of others. As the custodian of government funds and in part its financial agent, especially as to the management of the national debt, a royal charter, frequently altered and renewed, conferred on it certain privileges, among which was that of issuing notes, the circulation in 1895 amounting to some £27,000,000. Of coin and bullion about £25,000,000 is the average amount contained in its vaults, while its business exceeds £2,000,000 a day, and on its present capital of £14,553,000 are paid yearly dividends, usually of nine or ten per cent. All the gold bullion offered is bought at an unvarying rate; but for silver bullion it has little use, silver being legal tender only for payments not exceeding two pounds sterling. Opposite the bank, in Capel court, is the stock exchange, with nearly 3,500 members, and with daily transactions of fabulous amount. At the bankers clearing-house on Lombard street, a business of only £7,000,000,000 or £8,000,000,000 a year is considered as an indication of dull times and financial depression. In these three establishments is largely represented the wealth not only of Great Britain but of the world; for at the stock exchange are listed the securities of many foreign lands, and at the bank of England are held the reserves of many other banks, British, colonial, and European.

ST. PAUL'S CATHEDRAL, BLACKFRIARS BRIDGE

From Cheapside we pass into St. Paul's church-yard where, on the site of a chapel founded by King Aethelbert in 610, stands one of the largest ecclesiastical structures in the world. Destroyed by fire in 1087, the church was replaced by a Norman edifice, 730 feet long, and large enough, as William of Malmesbury declared, "to contain the utmost conceivable multitude of worshippers." In 1561 its steeple, more than 500 feet above ground, was struck by lightning, and the building partially destroyed, its restoration under Inigo Jones being still in progress at the time of the great fire which swept London out of existence. As rebuilt from the designs of Christopher Wren, at a cost of £748,000, the cathedral is of cruciform shape, 500 by 250 feet, and with a dome whose surmounting cross is more than 400 feet above the pavement. In front of the main facade, or rather forming a portion of it, is a double portico of Corinthian pillars; and at the transepts are semicircular rows, the tall campanile towers at two of the corners adding to the architectural effect. Of symmetrical proportions, and with massive simplicity of outline, it is an impressive rather than a pleasing composition, one dimmed with age, moreover, and with London smoke;

while surrounded as it is with houses and shops, its colossal dimensions can not be realized, except perhaps from Blackfriars bridge adjacent. The interior is imposing from its vastness, but dark and bare, except for a few embellishments in marble, mosaics, gilding, and stained glass. There are numerous statues and monuments, however, for here are the tombs of many whom England loves to honor; Nelson and Rodney, Wellington and the Napiers; Picton and Ponsonby, both of whom fell at Waterloo; Joshua Reynolds the painter, Hallam the historian, and dear old Samuel Johnson.

But Westminster abbey, with its long rows of monuments to the mighty dead, is regarded as the English temple of fame, and burial within its vaults, though not always worthily bestowed, is deemed as the greatest honor that the nation can bestow. Originally a chapel dedicated to St. Peter by King Siebert the Saxon, it was built on an islet overgrown with thorns, and thence termed Thorney isle. Connected with it was a Benedictine monasterium, or minster, west of the Cistercian abbey of St. Mary; and thus the name of Westminster. Destroyed by the Danes, it was re-erected by King Edgar, and again by Edward the Confessor, appearing when completed in 1065 almost as large as now it stands. The present structure, begun by Henry III in 1220, was practically finished by Edward I, but with additions and improvements, so-called, down to the time of Henry VII and even of Christopher Wren, by whom were built the two western towers. Its total length is 530 feet; the transepts are a little more than 200 feet in breadth; the nave and aisles having

WESTMINSTER ABBEY

a width of 75 feet. It is in the form of a Latin cross, and, for the most part of the early English style, but with traces of Norman and attempts at Gothic architecture. The interior is striking in effect, with symmetry of proportion and richness of coloring, especially in the triforium and the marble columns, though marred here and there by modern restorations and monuments in execrable taste.

The choir, with its fourteenth century decorations, where are held the coronation ceremonies of British sovereigns, is perhaps the most beautiful portion. In the north transept are the statues and busts of statesmen, warriors, and other famous men, as of the earl of Chatham, the younger Pitt, Fox, Palmerston, Beaconsfield, Warren Hastings, Richard Cobden, Isaac Newton, Lyell, and Darwin. In the aisles and chapels, that of Henry VII being remarkable for its fretted vault and beautiful tracery, are the monuments of kings and queens, of patriots, travellers, and men of science. In the south transept is the poet's corner, where are the memorials of famous writers from Chaucer to Charles Dickens, a prominent place being given to Shakespeare, whose figure stands on an altar-like pedestal, the right arm leaning on the volumes that contain his works, from which is selected, by way

SIR ISAAC NEWTON

of epitaph, his own immortal words:

> *We are such stuff as dreams are made of.*
> *And our little life is rounded with a sleep.*

In connection with Westminster abbey may be mentioned the school of that name, one of the most ancient of London's educational institutions, the old abbey dormitory serving as the principal school-room, while the dining-room tables were made, as is said, from the timbers of Spanish vessels of Philip's unfortunate armada.

The new palace of Westminster, built from Barry's designs for the houses of parliament, and forming with Westminster hall a single group, was begun in 1840 and completed in 1867 at a cost of £3,000,000, the site being that of a former palace destroyed by fire in 1835. It is of the later Gothic style, covering an area of nearly six acres, and of imposing aspect, especially the facade that fronts on the river, 940 feet long and with rich and tasteful decorative scheme. The central hall, entered from St. Stephen's porch and surmounted by a dome and lofty spire, separates the house of lords from the house of commons; at the northeast corner is a campanile tower resembling that of the cathedral of Bruges, and above the royal entrance is the Victoria tower, 340 feet in height. Though

WESTMINSTER ABBEY, HOUSES OF PARLIAMENT

perhaps the finest and certainly the most elaborate of London edifices, it has serious structural defects, the stone-work gradually crumbling away, while the level is so low that its basement is beneath the high-water mark of the Thames.

There are 100 stairways and 1,100 apartments in the various buildings, all the rooms being handsomely furnished and equipped, some in magnificent style and at lavish expense. Ascending the principal staircase, we pass through a Norman porch, to the right of which is the queen's robing room, richly adorned with carvings and paintings of allegorical subjects, and of Arthurian and other legends. Adjoining it is the Victoria gallery, with pavement of mosaic work, panelled and gilded ceiling, and on the sides frescos by Maclise, representing the death of Nelson and the meeting of Wellington and Blucher at the close of

Waterloo. It is from this gallery that the queen proceeds, or rather used to proceed, to the house of peers, when about to prorogue or open parliament.

The chamber of the peers is oblong in shape, its walls and ceiling finely decorated, its stained-glass windows covered with portraits of English monarchs, and its floor almost filled with the red leather benches provided for the members. At the southern end of the chamber, beneath a gilded canopy and flanked by gilt candelabra, is the royal throne of England, with those of the late prince consort and the prince of Wales on either side. The canopy is in three compartments, the central portion beautifully panelled, with lions passant carved and gilded on a crimson ground, and above them the royal arms and the motto "Dieu et Mon Droit" on a band of deep blue. At some distance in front is the woolsack of the lord-chancellor, resembling a cushioned ottoman, and at the end opposite the throne is the bar, where messages are received from the commons. Adjacent are the peers' lobby and corridor, leading into the central hall, with stone vaulting inlaid with Venetian mosaics, representing the heraldic emblems of the crown, and whence a second corridor and lobby lead into the house of commons, a spacious chamber fitted and furnished in substantial business-like fashion.

HOUSE OF LORDS

LOBBY, HOUSE OF COMMONS

Westminster hall, forming the vestibule of the houses of parliament, is a portion of the palace founded by William Rufus, and enlarged and occupied by Saxon kings and their successors until the days of Henry VIII. It is nearly 300 feet in length and more than 90 in height, its ceiling unsupported by columns, and its carved oaken roof a masterpiece of constructive skill. Here were held some of the first of English parliaments, and later the festivals which followed the coronation of English monarchs. In other respects it is rich in historic interest; for here it was that Charles I was condemned to death and that Cromwell was saluted as lord-protector, while William Wallace, Thomas More, Strafford, Warren Hastings, and others were arraigned for trial at its bar. In the old palace yard is an equestrian statue of Richard the Lion-hearted; in the new palace yard are bronze statues of Palmerston, Derby, Peel, and Canning; and in Parliament square is one of Beaconsfield attired in the robes of the garter.

CROMWELL

Of the once famous abode of royalty known as Whitehall palace, almost destroyed by fire near the close of the seventeenth century, only the banqueting chamber now remains. The original building, with its valuable contents, was presented by Hubert de Burgh to the Dominican brotherhood, by whom it was sold to the archbishop of York, and thenceforth, until the downfall of Wolsey, became the residence of the archbishops of York, under the name of York palace. But, says Shakespeare in his Henry VIII:

> *Since the cardinal fell, that title's lost;*
> *'Tis now the king's, and called — Whitehall.*

The banqueting hall, through which Charles I passed to execution, and where Charles II held his profligate court, is a spacious and lofty apartment, its ceiling adorned with allegorical and other paintings by Rubens. Converted into a chapel by George in 1694, it became the headquarters of the United Service museum, in which is an interesting collection relating to the military and naval professions, including a model of Waterloo representing nearly 200,000 figures. After the destruction of Whitehall, St. James's palace became the royal residence, until in 1809 it suffered a similar fate, except its gateway, its chapel, and its presence chamber, in which are many valuable portraits and other works of art. Though no longer held here, it is from this palace that the British court is still known as the court of St. James's.

Buckingham palace, on the western extremity of St. James's park, is the town residence of Queen Victoria. Built by John Sheffield, duke of Buckingham, it was purchased and occasionally occupied by George III; but though remodelled by Nash during the reign of his successor, remained for the most part tenantless until selected as the mansion of the present sovereign in the year of her coronation. A wing 460 feet in length, a large ball-room, and other apartments were later added, the entire group forming a quadrangle by no means remarkable for beauty of design. The sculpture and picture galleries, the former entered through a portico of marble columns, are the most attractive features, containing a fine collection by Dutch and other masters, as Rembrandt, Teniers, Rubens, Van Dyck, Jan Steen, Paul Potter, and Van Ruysdael. In the dining-room are portraits of English sovereigns, some of them by Gainsborough, and in an adjoining chamber are Cimabue's 'Madonna' and Leighton's 'Procession in Florence.'

BUCKINGHAM PALACE

The ball and concert rooms, reached from a marble stairway embellished with Townsend's frescos, are handsome apartments, their walls bordered with seats draped in satin. Beyond is the throne-room, where the queen receives her guests in state, a magnificent chamber upholstered in gilding and red striped velvet, its marble frieze, beneath a vaulted and richly decorated ceiling, adorned with reliefs whose subject is the wars of the Roses. The green drawing-room is another famous apartment; in the garden is a summer-house with frescos by Landseer, Eastlake, Maclise, and others, representing scenes from Milton's *Comus*; nor should we forget the royal mews; that is to say the stable and coach-houses, with accommodation for forty equipages, the state carriage, built in 1762, costing nearly £8,000. The queen is by no means extravagant in her entertainments, the cost of state concerts never exceeding £3,000, and of state balls £2,000, or less than would suffice for the purchase of flowers if given by a New York millionaire.

The queen has other mansions, among which is Windsor castle, some twenty miles from London, and but a short distance from Eton college, the most famous of English schools, and for centuries a favorite institution among the wealthy and titled classes. Founded by William the Conqueror, on a hill which centres amid an estate originally belonging to Edward the Confessor, the castle, after being several times extended, was rebuilt by William of Wyckham, and after further extensions and restorations, was completed in the reign of Victoria at a cost of £900,000. From the terraces which surround it broad flights of steps lead to a tasteful flower garden embellished with statuary, and from the battlements of the Round tower, or keep, near the Norman gate, is an excellent view of the broad reaches of the Thames, and of a landscape embracing some of the fairest of English scenery.

WINDSOR CASTLE

In the audience chamber, the presence chamber, the throne-room and grand reception room are many valuable paintings and tapestries, the last being decorated in rococo style and containing malachite and other vases presented by European monarchs. In the guard chamber, above whose mantelpiece is a silver shield inlaid with gold presented by Francis I to Henry VIII, there are suits of old armor with busts and relics of famous generals and admirals; the Waterloo chamber, which is also the grand dining-room, being adorned, as are most of the apartments with portraits, statues, and other works of art. In the private rooms is one of the finest collections extant of gold and silver plate, of oriental and Sevres chinaware, of medieval cabinets, of bibliographical treasures, and of drawings and miniatures by Raphael, Michael Angelo, Holbein, and Leonardo da Vinci. In St. George's chapel, a fifteenth century structure with fan-shaped vaulted roof, near the gateway of Henry VIII, are some beautiful effects in carving, sculpture, and stained-glass windows. Adjoining it is the Albert chapel, formerly belonging to Wolsey, and restored by the queen in honor of the late prince consort, its interior embellished with colored marbles, mosaics, gildings, and precious stones in rich and varied profusion; for the queen loves the memory of her husband more than all the world beside.

Osborne house in the isle of Wight is another of Victoria's residences; and still another, and best beloved of all, is Balmoral castle, on the bank of Dee, of which mention will be made in connection with Scottish annals. Marlborough house, erected for the first duke of Marlborough from the designs of Christopher Wren, was occupied in 1863 as the city residence of the prince of Wales, of whose country seat at Sandringham hall I have spoken elsewhere in this work.

ST. THOMAS HOSPITAL

Adjacent to St. Thomas hospital, on the southern bank of Thames, is Lambeth palace, for more than six centuries the residence of the archbishops of Canterbury. Its oldest portion is the chapel erected by Archbishop Boniface in 1245, the screen and windows being contributions from Archbishop Laud, while the Lollards' tower adjoining is so called because these disciples of Wycliffe were imprisoned and tortured in its keep. Here also were confined the poet Lovelace, Thomas Armstrong, and Queen Elizabeth's favorite, the earl of Essex. Among the art treasures of the palace are portraits of all the archbishops of Canterbury since 1533, and in its library, established by Archbishop Bancroft in 1610, are 35,000 volumes and more than 2,000 manuscripts, including some of the most valuable of ecclesiastical documents.

EARL OF ESSEX

To the British museum, with its various galleries of antiquities, it is impossible here to make other than brief reference. Of its origin, through the purchase in 1753 of the Sloane collection of books and manuscripts, I have already spoken. In 1896 the library contained over 1,750,000 volumes and 60,000 manuscripts, with a yearly increment of 10,000 to 12,000 works. It consists in truth of many libraries, some preserved in separate compartments, and some absorbed among the general in-gathering. While far from complete, even as to English literature, it is without a rival in catholicity of scope, and contains a large number of rarities. In the United States there are few that can compare with it in the productions of American authors; it has the best Dutch library outside of Holland, the best Hungarian library outside of Hungary, and the best Slavonic library apart from the Imperial collection at St Petersburg, while in the Hebrew, Chinese, and other oriental languages there are more than 50,000 volumes. The manuscripts date from the second century before Christ, and include the famous Alexandrian collection, the chronicles of Anglo-Saxon kings, and the written legends of the Arthurian romance. There are marvels of gold-letter and illuminated works, among them Archbishop Bede's copy of the book of Durham and the celebrated Bedford missal, with Sanskrit, Hebrew, Syriac, Arabian, and other oriental documents, to say nothing of royal charters and genealogical pedigrees.

In the bronze and vase rooms of the museum are some of the rarest of classic and mediaeval treasures, including Roman vessels of silver, and a silver ministerium or service of third century workmanship. In the medal and gold ornament chambers are gold and silver coins from 700 B.C. to the time of the Roman empire, arranged in chronological order, besides many others of later date, with golden ornaments, cameos, and gems of priceless value. Then there is the famous Portland or Barberini vase of dark blue glass, beautifully decorated with reliefs, unearthed from a Roman tomb early in the seventeenth century, and becoming the property of Prince Barberini before it was purchased by the duke of Portland.

The National gallery, the largest of the buildings fronting on Trafalgar square, was erected some threescore years ago on the site of a royal stable at a cost of £95,000, but with recent alterations and enlargements costing as much more. Of its contents, the nucleus was formed through the purchase by parliament, in 1824, of the Angerstein collection; and to this many additions have been made, both by purchase and bequest. While all the principal schools are well represented in its twenty-two departments, it is strong in the works of English masters, an entire chamber being devoted to the canvases of Turner, one of the greatest of landscape painters. Of many private collections, perhaps the most famous are those in the mansions of the duke of Westminster and the earl of Ellesmere. The Royal academy of fine arts, founded in 1768, and whose present quarters are at Burlington house, one of the finest specimens of the Italian renaissance, holds annual exhibitions, together with classes for instruction. In the Grosvenor gallery, by the society of painters in water colors, and by the society of British artists, exhibitions are also held. The South Kensington museum contains one of the finest art collections in the world, both as to value and extent. It has also a department of applied or decorative art, with training schools, a collection of 250,000 drawings, engravings, and photographs, and large libraries pertaining to the various branches taught or illustrated in its several divisions.

In conclusion, let us turn for a moment to the drama, of whose growth and development a brief glance may be of interest. In the twelfth century, says William Fitzstephen, a Canterbury monk and mediaeval historian, London, "instead of showes upon theatres and comical pastimes, had holy plays and representations of miracles." In 1409 a play lasting eight days was acted, having for its subject "all matter from the creation of the world," and it was not until late in this century that the sacred began to give way to the secular drama. In the days of Shakespeare, who wrote divinely but played indifferently, his own ghost in *Hamlet* being the best of his parts, there were several theatres, chief among which were the Blackfriars and the Globe. Drury Lane was built somewhat later, and was burned in 1672, at which time there was in Dorset gardens a theatre designed by Christopher Wren, which Dryden describes as "like Nero's palace shining all with gold." This, however, is mere poetic license, except perhaps as to a little gilding; for the entire cost did not exceed £8,000. It was here that opera was first given in London, in 1673, the Haymarket, Covent Garden, and Her Majesty's being its later homes.

In 1897 the metropolis contained more than 30 respectable theatres and a large number of music halls, most of which may be classed as respectable, except as to the exposure of the female form, which has now gone so far that it cannot well go further; for indecent exposure here is at once suppressed by the Lord chamberlain, though not as yet at fashionable theatres, balls, and dinner parties. London pavilion is one of the best; and the Albert hall, used also for other purposes, is the largest of the better class, altogether too large for its acoustic properties, and with other faults that impair the effect of orchestral and choral performances. The same remark applies to the Crystal and Alexandra palaces, the former having at times a seated audience of 25,000 persons. Constructed at a cost of £1,500,000, chiefly of the glass and iron contained in the Exhibition building of 1851, it is beautifully situated in the suburb of Sydenham on an elevated site of 200 acres laid out in

CRYSTAL PALACE

the finest style of landscape art. The Alexandra palace has similar advantages, and in both are scientific and art collections, all of which with many other attractions, including a pleasant trip by rail, are offered to the public at a nominal fee.

Such are a few among the sights of London, a few only of the countless forms in which wealth is embodied or contained, its suburbs and suburban towns alone, such as Greenwich, Richmond, Kew, and Hampton court, with its stately palace and handsome grounds, containing more wealth than many cities that are accounted rich. In no city in the world is there so much opulence, and in none is there so much poverty, the income of the various charitable institutions amounting to nearly £5,000,000 a year, while large amounts

HAMPTON COURT

are distributed in parish relief. As to the aggregate value of property no reliable estimate can be formed; but it is far in the thousands of millions; for except in occasional seasons of adversity, commerce has been gradually swelling the total ever since the Roman occupation, when Bede spoke of the city as already "the mart of many nations resorting to it by sea and land." Enjoying as it does a virtual monopoly of the trade of China and the East Indies, the imports of the metropolis are far in excess of exports, 250,000,000 pounds of tea, for instance, being taken each twelvemonth for consumption and distribution, while of cereals, wool, tobacco, wines and liquors, coffee, cocoa, sugar, and other commodities the receipts are on an enormous scale. Of the entire imports and exports of the United Kingdom, averaging about £700,000,000 a year, nearly one-third pass through the port of London, while the tonnage of vessels entering and clearing is not short of 14,000,000, and there are more than 2,000 acres of docks. Manufactures are on a considerable scale, among the leading industries being foundries and engineering works, tanneries, pottery and glass-works, chemical and paper-works; but breweries lead all the rest, the establishment of Barclay Perkins and company, belonging at one time to Thrale, the friend of Samuel Johnson covering an area of thirteen acres.

Metropolitan society, like the metropolis itself, is on a huge and unwieldy scale, including a vast number and variety of cliques and sets, with a few real social leaders and with innumerable pretenders. As to the forces which sway these social organizations, the most powerful among them is wealth, London, in common with New York and other American cities, bring now under the domination of a plutocracy rather than of an aristocracy. Of this plutocracy one of the strongest elements is the Hebraic; for the Hebrews not only form the richest class, but are regarded with special favor by the prince of Wales, who is at the head of the social system. The Rothschilds, of whom mention has before been made, are no less puissant as social than as financial potentates. The brothers entertain freely and in magnificent style, especially Alfred, the second as to age, the heir-apparent being one of his familiar guests. All are liberal patrons of literature and art, giving freely of their abundance toward the support of public institutions, and also to the cause of charity. Many are those who are indebted to the Rothschilds for their fortunes, and none who have placed their trust in them ever found just cause for reproach.

LORD ROTHSCHILD

The duke of Westminster is one of the richest men in England, and one of the richest in the world, with a fortune estimated at $175,000,000, and an income of $5,000,000 a year. His wealth consists, moreover, of that most stable of all investments, real estate; mainly in the city of London, where he is known as the landlord of the West end, owning more than a thousand stately mansions and a number of the most valuable business blocks in this fashionable quarter of the world's greatest metropolis. His own mansion, Eaton hall, is itself a group of palatial edifices; more costly and magnificent than those which belong to the queen, and containing many treasures of art and articles of virtu. Among his possessions are 125,000 acres of forest and

EATON HALL, CHESHIRE

moorland in Scotland, where he passes much of his time in hunting; for though well stricken in years, he is one of the keenest of sportsmen. He has also the finest stable and stud farms in Great Britain, his horses being several times winners of the Derby, the most highly prized of all the honors of the turf. For admission to his art gallery the duke charges a small fee, devoting the proceeds to charity; and in this connection the following story is told; true, no doubt, though somewhat commonplace, similar incidents having been applied to many other important personages. A visitor entering the grounds not long ago, met there an elderly man attired in a plain tweed shooting-jacket and other garments to match. He asked to be shown through the mansion, or such portions of as was permitted, and to this the other readily agreed, conducting him through the various buildings and showing him all that was best worth seeing. So obliging was the guide that he received half a crown for his services, and this he slipped into his pocket without saying a word. A few days later the visitor learned that his cicerone was the duke of Westminster.

DUKE OF WESTMINSTER

Among other wealthy noble men is the duke of Fife, who, though a Scotchman, spends much of his time in London. In addition to his revenues from 300,000 acres of land, a large slice from the small isles of Britain, he has a large income from banks in which he is partner, and railways and industrial enterprises in which he is a director. His investments are usually fortunate, some founders shares, for example, purchased not many years ago for £30 selling as is related for £40,000. Yet his wife, the princess Louise, who may become queen of Great Britain and empress of India, makes her own dresses and hats, and like her mother, the princess of Wales, is in manners and habits one of the most sincere of women.

To the south of London are the most ancient and attractive of English country towns, while to the north are the most wealthy and populous, especially those in the manufacturing districts. To the former class belongs Canterbury, a quaint little city with less than 25,000 inhabitants, but since the days of Becket the ecclesiastical capital of England, its archbishop being not only primate but metropolitan of all the dioceses south of the Trent. The cathedral stands on the site of the Roman chapel which King Aethelbert presented, together with his own palace, to St. Augustine and his missionary band, Augustine himself being the first of its dignitaries and Archibald Tait, the present archbishop, the ninety-third in succession. The choir was rebuilt by Anselm and restored and enlarged after the fire of 1172, virtually as it stands to-day. It is 180 feet long, the screen which separates it from the nave, flanked by grand Norman arches supported on massive piers, being of fifteenth century workmanship. The nave and transepts are similar in style, well lighted and of comparatively modern design. It was in the northwestern transept that Becket was murdered, the spot still showing the mark of the altar erected in commemoration of the tragedy. At the eastern end of the choir aisles and approached by flights of steps is

CANTERBURY

CATHEDRAL, CANTERBURY

Trinity chapel, where was the shrine of the martyred prelate, so richly decorated that, as Erasmus declares, "gold was the meanest thing about it." Destroyed by order of Henry VIII, and its treasures confiscated, no trace of it now remains, except upon the surrounding pavement worn by the knees of many pilgrims. Among the monuments of this chapel are those of Henry IV and Edward the Black prince, above whose brazen effigy are his gauntlets, shield, and helmet.

Of Gravesend, Chatham, Rochester, and other towns near the mouth of Thames, I need not stop to speak, though Rochester is an episcopal city, its cathedral as well as the remnants of its castle being of ancient Norman architecture. To the south-east of it lies the port of Dover, also with its ancient castle, now converted into a fort, opposite the western heights which culminate in Shakespeare's cliff. Of old Dover, the Dubris of the Romans, little now remains; but of the Norman period there is much to remind us, especially in the church beneath Castle hill. Its harbor has several basins, used chiefly by the mail steamers which ply across the channel, and the admiralty pier is a massive structure extending for a third of a mile into the strait. There are several rows of neat and commodious residences, especially in the visitors' quarter; for Dover is a popular, if not a fashionable watering-place.

The southern and southeastern shores of England are skirted with watering-places, beginning with Margate, almost on the estuary of the Thames, and thence westward to the Cornish coast. Chief among them are Ramsgate, Hastings, Brighton, Worthing, and Bournemouth, and on the isle of Wight the town of Cowes, whose port is the headquarters of the royal yacht squadron. On the eastern coast Scarborough and Whitby are the favorite resorts, and on the west there are Blackpool, Llandudno, and Aberystwyth. All have their attractions; though Brighton and Scarborough are most in favor, both having excellent drives, promenades, and piers, in sight of which are the boldest of cliffs, and the finest of marine landscapes, while their hotels, shops, and theatres are among the best outside of

SCARBOROUGH

the metropolis. Some forty miles south of Scarborough is Hull, or Kingston-upon-Hull, the principal seaport of the eastern coast, and with a commerce surpassed only by that of London and Liverpool.

Plymouth and Southampton are the chief commercial and shipping ports on the southern coast. The former is picturesquely situated on the sound of that name, its harbor protected by one of the finest breakwaters in the World and spacious enough to afford anchorage for the entire British navy. It was here that the English fleet awaited the approach of the armada, the town itself furnishing seven of the ships. There are several handsome thoroughfares lined with imposing business blocks; the public buildings are neat and substantial, and the residence quarters suggestive of wealth and comfort. Southampton has many beautiful villas and mansions, though in its ancient quarter is much of the antique, with narrow, tortuous streets, beyond which are remnants of the wall erected in the days of Richard II. The docks are extensive; for here are the headquarters of many steamship lines, more than 20,000 steam and sailing vessels entering or clearing yearly from this port. A few miles distant is Portsmouth, the chief naval station of England, with its huge government dockyard, begun by Henry VII, and now covering nearly 300 acres, the total cost exceeding £5,000,000, though largely constructed with convict labor.

Liverpool next to London is the largest of English seaports, the aggregate tonnage of its shipping exceeding 10,000,000 a year, while in volume of exports it far surpasses the metropolis. Its docks extend for many miles on either side of the Mersey, and year by year are being still further extended to meet the increasing demands of commerce. Their revenues are about £1,500,000 a year, sufficient, after meeting expenses, to pay interest on £18,000,000 of outstanding debt, which is but a portion of their cost. The Alexandra dock is the largest, with a water area of 45 acres, and it is here that most of the transatlantic steamers find accommodation. In common with the Waterloo dock, it is largely used by grain-laden vessels, and in the neighborhood of both are huge storehouses for grain. The landing stage for steamships consists of an enormous floating quay, more than 2,000 feet in length and connected with the shore by several bridges. Liverpool is not an attractive city, but it is an extremely busy one; its corn exchange largely regulating the price of grain throughout the world. The town-hall, costing £410,000, and the new exchange are among the finest of the public buildings; but the architectural feature of the city is St. George's hall, with its polished granite columns, its marble pavements, and its porticos of Corinthian pillars 60 feet in height. Bristol once ranked next to London as a seaport, and is still fourth on the list as to receipt of customs revenues. It is an ancient and interesting city, famous for ecclesiastical architecture, though many of the finest specimens have been destroyed. Connecting it with its sightly suburb of Clifton is the famous suspension bridge erected by Brunel, with a span of 700 feet and a roadway 250 feet above high-water mark.

CANNING DOCK, LIVERPOOL

ST. GEORGE'S HALL, LIVERPOOL

Proceeding eastward from Liverpool, and a little toward the north and south, we come to such manufacturing towns as Manchester, Oldham, and Preston; Leeds, Bradford, and Huddersfield; Sheffield and a score of others. To some brief reference has already been made; and as to the rest it need only be said that, except as wealth-producing centres, there is nothing about them of interest, tall chimneys vomiting forth the clouds of smoke which settle like a pall in the surrounding atmosphere, making them the dreariest and dirtiest among the abodes of man. Much cleaner are such manufacturing towns as Nottingham and Coventry, the former noted for its hosiery, as the place where Arkwright fashioned the first spinning frame, and to which Hargreaves removed with his spinning jenny after being driven by a mob from Blackburn. Ribbons and watchmaking are the chief industries of Coventry, so named from the Benedictine convent founded in 1043 by Earl Leofric and his wife, the lady Godiva, the latter celebrated in Tennyson's poem as riding through the city streets "clothed on with chastity." It is a city of churches, the oldest of which, St. Michael's, with a steeple more than 300 feet high, is among the finest specimens of architecture on perpendicular lines.

In addition to those already mentioned, there are several cathedral towns in England, one of the oldest of which is York, the Eboracum of the Roman period, its ancient walls still partially surrounding the narrow, crooked streets, overhung here and there with the quaint old-fashioned houses of mediaeval days. Its minster or cathedral, originally a small wooden chapel built by the first archbishop of York in 627, is a noble specimen of church architecture. Especially fine is the effect of the western front, its sections corresponding with the nave and aisles, and above the entrance a large window whose foliated tracery is one of the most beautiful specimens of fourteenth century workmanship. The transepts and crypt, belonging to the twelfth and thirteenth centuries, are the oldest portion of the building; and the main transept is considered as the gem of this stately composition, though in the south transept, with its rich rose window, is more elaboration of detail. St. Mary's abbey, or that which remains of it, is also a structure of historic interest, its hospitium being used as a museum of antiquities. There are many time-honored churches, and among secular buildings the guild-hall, the mansion-house, and the assembly rooms are the most remarkable. Of the castle, now used as a prison, the oldest portion is Clifford's tower, formerly the donjon of the Norman fortress erected by William the Conqueror.

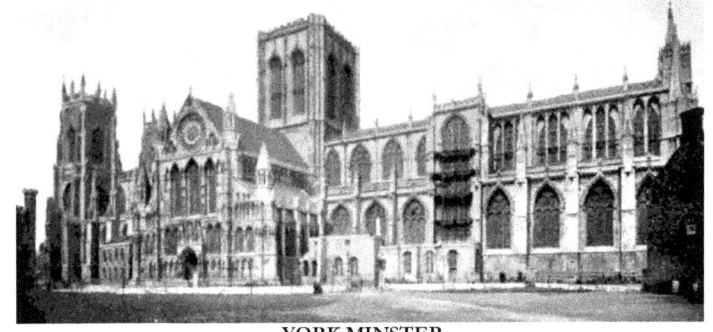

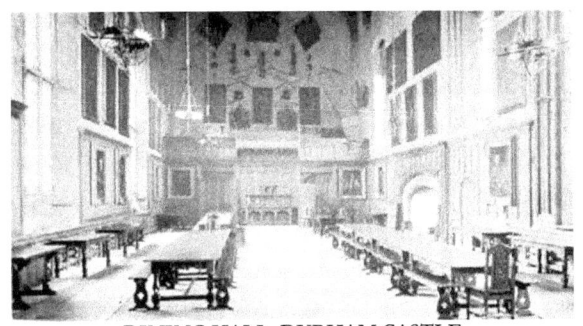

Of Durham cathedral, its ancient Norman church still forms the principal portion; and though there have been many additions, the interior, with its massive pillars and arches, is almost perfect in its magnificent proportions and decorative features. Its dimensions are almost the same as those of York minster, — 510 feet in length by 200 in breadth, and with a central tower 215 feet in height. In the Galilee chapel, completed in 1195, the remains of Bede lie at rest; and in the chapel of the Nine Altars are those of St. Cuthbert. The see of Durham was formerly the richest in England, its revenues amounting to £37,000 a year; but in 1836 the income of the prelate was reduced to £8,000 and the surplus applied toward increasing the stipends of poorer bishops. Durham castle, with its great hall constructed by Bishop Hatfield, its Norman hall, chapels, and other apartments, is now the headquarters of a university which ranks among the foremost of England's educational institutions.

Of all English cities Chester is the only one that retains its ancient walls in their entirety, though with gateways rebuilt toward the close of the eighteenth century. It is a quaint little town, the four principal streets radiating at right angles from the market cross and terminating at the gates. They are flanked by what are termed "rows," serving as sidewalks but boarded or flagged and ceiled, thus forming a covered way, behind which are houses and shops with overhanging roofs. The origin of these rows is still in controversy; but the effect is unique, and in conjunction with the old-fashioned buildings, strikingly picturesque. The cathedral, formerly the abbey church of St. Werburgh, dating from the early Saxon period, is of composite architecture, the choir with its rich marble flooring, its beautifully carved stalls, and its altar of cedar and olive from the groves of Palestine forming its most attractive feature.

CHESTER

Lincoln cathedral, it is said, was the earliest building in Europe of purely Gothic design, and though now combining many varieties of style, is not surpassed even by York minster in grandeur of effect and elegance of detail. Its symmetry of proportion shows to the best advantage, crowning as it does the hill on which the city is built; its central tower, 260 feet high and supported by lofty arches with massive stone piers, giving accentuation to the plan. In the interior the presbytery and the choir stalls with their antique carvings are among the finest specimens of human workmanship, and though most of the stained-glass windows are modern and in doubtful taste, there are some which are beautifully decorated, especially the one in the east transept, and that which is known as "the Bishop's eye." Apart from its cathedral Lincoln has much of historic interest; for here on the site of its minster and of a castle erected by William the Conqueror, stood, at least as early as 100 A.D., the Roman settlement which Bede calls Lindocolina. It was in this castle that Matilda was besieged by King Stephen, that the first of the Plantagenets was crowned, and that David I of Scotland did homage to King John. Though a small city, it has many costly residences and public buildings, while from time immemorial it has been a parliamentary borough.

LINCOLN CATHEDRAL

Of Worcester, as of Lincoln, the cathedral is its pride and glory, the see of the former being established in 780, after which date the bishop's church of St. Peter's was absorbed in the monastery of St. Mary, the canons turning monks, and thus was later established a monastic cathedral. Bishop Wulfstan, the only Saxon prelate whom the

Norman conquerors left in possession of his diocese, erected here a church, of which portions are embodied in the present building; and after his canonization the rich offerings at his shrine permitted its conversion into a cathedral, the lady chapel being a later addition, as are the chapter-house and the refectory, now used as a Grammar school, the entire structure being remodelled about the middle of the present century at a cost of £100,000. The choir is exceedingly beautiful; its slender marble shafts with capitals most delicately carved, and contrasting somewhat with the profusely decorated screen. Among the monuments is that of Bishop Gauden, the real author of the *Icon Basilike*, wrongly attributed to Charles I, while the sepulchral effigy of King John is probably the earliest of its kind. Across College green, near which stood Worcester castle, are the remains of the Guesten hall, formerly a portion of the Benedictine priory once connected with the cathedral.

Other cathedrals might here be mentioned, as those of Exeter and Winchester with their beautiful choirs and altar screens, Ely and Wells, the former one of the largest in England, Lichfield and Peterborough, both rich in historic associations, Salisbury with its spacious transept, and Gloucester with its elaborate ornamentation; but sufficient has been said to indicate the general character of church architecture and decoration as it exists in England in its highest forms. Finally, some reference is needed to the university towns of Oxford and Cambridge, which as seats of learning rank above all others in the British isles, except Trinity college, Dublin, though not requiring detailed description.

EXETER CATHEDRAL

While the seat of a wealthy diocese, and famed through many historic associations, Oxford, that is to say — "the ford for oxen," as appears from its eleventh century name of Oxenford, is noted mainly for its colleges, on which the town largely depends for the support of its 55,000 inhabitants. It is a beautiful city, surrounded by an amphitheatre of hills, stately towers, and spires rising from ancient quadrangles, from cloistered gardens, and from groves of oak more ancient than the mediaeval buildings around which they are clustered. In connection with the university may first be mentioned the Bodleian library, founded in 1602 by Thomas Bodley, and now containing about 500,000 volumes and 35,000 manuscripts, including the finest collection extant of oriental documents, and of the earliest editions of the Greek and Latin classics. It has also the right to receive a copy of every book that is published in the United Kingdom; these are housed in the Radcliffe library, founded by a physician of that name who, dying in 1714, bequeathed for that purpose £40,000, together with an income for its support.

The university of Oxford contains 21 colleges, nearly 100 professors or lecturers, several hundred fellows and tutors, and about 3,000 students. It is the largest and wealthiest educational institution in England, bequests and endowments accumulating for several centuries and affording a princely revenue, largely distributed in scholarships and fellowships varying in value from a nominal sum to as much as £1,000 a year. He who secures a fellowship retains it as a rule for life, or so long as he remains unmarried; for the supposition is that one who can support a wife should first be able to support himself; moreover, except as occasional visitors, women are regarded as a drawback to serious study and otherwise out of place. University, Balliol, Oriel, Exeter, and Queen's are the oldest of Oxford colleges, and Christ's, founded by Cardinal Wolsey in 1524, is one of the largest and most fashionable. The cathedral of the diocese serves as its chapel, and though the smallest in England is one of the most ornate, its choir stalls and episcopal throne being of elaborate workmanship, while its windows by Burne Jones are among the finest of his compositions. Brasenose, whose name is derived from a door-knocker belonging to an older institution, though itself founded in 1509, is noted rather for its athletes and boating-men than for its students, furnishing some of the stoutest contestants in the annual race with Cambridge.

CARDINAL WOLSEY

Though less wealthy and fashionable than Oxford colleges, those of Cambridge are not inferior to the sister university in scholarship, nor in the list of eminent men numbered among their graduates. The largest colleges are Trinity and St. John's, the former established by Henry VIII as a consolidation of several ancient foundations. Its large rectangular court is profusely adorned with statuary, and in its hall are the portraits of such eminent alumni as Bacon, Newton, and Dryden, while Byron, Macaulay, Thackeray, and Tennyson are also among those to whom Trinity was an alma mater. At King's college, also completed by Henry VIII, but founded by Henry VI, the two Walpoles, Richard

KING'S COLLEGE, CAMBRIDGE

Temple, Stratford de Redcliffe, and many others known to fame completed their education. The chapel of King's with its vaulted ceiling, its carved stalls, and its handsome altarpiece and organ screen is one of the finest in Cambridge. Near the ancient gateway of King's is Clare, with modern buildings though one of the oldest colleges in the group.

Proceeding westward from Herefordshire into the adjoining Welsh counties of Brecknock and Radnor, we find there, separated only two or three miles from English communities, a people who cannot even speak their language, one having nothing in common with the English except that both are subject to the same government. To the larger towns of Wales this remark does not of course apply; but in the country, and especially in the mountainous districts, there are many families still living almost in the same condition as when the Keltic tribes from which they are descended were driven westward by the Roman legions. They are an industrious and thrifty folk, but extremely superstitious and averse to change of whatever kind. They will not milk their cows on Sunday; for this they account as sinful; and still are worn by women the tall sugar-loaf hats bequeathed as heirlooms from one generation to another, and not considered respectable until much the worse for wear.

While the northern portion of Wales is extremely mountainous, there are in the central and southern counties large areas of cultivable and pasture land, 60 per cent of its surface being thus classified against only 25 per cent in Scotland. Nevertheless there are many districts almost worthless for farming purposes, where the soil is barren and the rains so excessive that not one crop of hay out of three is gathered in serviceable condition. With live-stock the country is fairly supplied, and especially with sheep, which thrive where cattle and horses would starve; yet of the agricultural holdings more than half are of less than 20 acres, and there are many thousands of less than five acres. The land is rich in minerals, with deposits of coal and iron not inferior to those of England, and it is in these deposits and the manufactures fostered thereby that the wealth of the country mainly consists.

Cardiff, so-called from its caer or castle, an eleventh century structure but with modern restorations, especially in its frescoed banqueting hall, ships every year more than 10,000,000 tons of coal, in addition to large quantities of raw and manufactured iron. It has six miles of quays and 115 acres of docks, most of the latter constructed by the marquis of Bute, to whom, as lord of the manor, the town owes much of its prosperity. Some 40 miles to the west is Swansea, which has been termed the metallurgical centre of the world; and though this title may be exaggerated, it is not so with reference to copper,

CARDIFF CASTLE

which is sent here to be smelted from many foreign lands, though not a pound of that metal is found in this portion of Wales. Iron, lead, tin-plate, zinc, and other manufacturing works are on an extensive scale, and in the neighborhood some 250 coal-pits afford an abundance of cheap fuel. Commerce is considerable, exports of tin-plate alone being valued at £3,000,000 a year.

Merthyr-Tydvil, noted for its iron and steel works, lies in the centre of the great coal basin of southern Wales. Newport, a few miles east from Cardiff, is a commercial and railroad centre with a moderate shipping trade. In the north are Bangor and Carnarvon, both lively and pleasant little towns, the former with a cathedral built on the site of a sixth century church; the latter with a castle founded in 1283, and one of the best preserved of mediaeval fortresses. Near Bangor are the Menai suspension and Britannia tubular bridges, the former completed in 1824 and regarded at the time as the greatest engineering achievement of the age. Among watering places are Aberystwyth, Tenby, and Llandudno; nor should we forget the seaport of Milford, whose spacious and land-locked harbor was believed to be the only one with depth of water sufficient for the *Great Eastern*, when loaded with her full cargo of 25,000 ton.

Since 1603, when the two crowns were united, and especially since 1705, when the two parliaments were united, Scotland and England have been virtually one nation, though never one people; for the Scotch are among the proudest of races, and strongly attached to their own customs and institutions. Certain it is that on the score of wealth they have nothing to complain of as to the results of this union; within the last two centuries the increase has been enormous, in much greater ratio probably than in southern Britain. For 1695 the entire rents of Scotland, whether in town or country, did not exceed £350,000; for 1895 they were estimated at more than £20,000,000; a gain of nearly sixty-fold, and about fifteen times greater than the proportionate gain in population. While this is caused in part by the smaller purchasing power of money and by a fictitious advance in rents, it is due more to improvements in agricultural methods, to the unfolding of mineral resources, and to the development of manufactures. The production of coal is at the rate of nearly 30,000,000 tons a year, and of iron and other metals the output is very considerable. The making of cloth and carpets, woollen and cotton fabrics keeps busy hundreds of factories and hundreds of thousands of operatives; there are sugar refineries, paper-mills, glass-works, pottery works, and countless other branches of industry; but most profitable of all is the distillation of whiskey, of which at least 25,000,000 gallons a year are produced in highland and other stills.

Glasgow is the industrial and commercial centre of Scotland, rivalling Manchester in its manufactures, Liverpool in its shipping trade, and ranking next to London in population. In shipbuilding, and especially the building of steel and iron vessels, it surpasses all other ports, the shipbuilding yards extending westward to Greenock, several miles beyond the city limits. Here are constructed or supplied with machinery two-thirds of the steamers that carry the British flag, including the largest and fastest of ocean and river craft, the number averaging 250 to 300 a year, with a burden of 350,000 to 400,000 tons. In improving the harbor and building docks more than £5,000,000 have been expended within the last half century; increasing the width of the Clyde by continual dredging from 180 to 450 feet, and its depth from three to 28 feet; at least 12,000 vessels belonging to all the nations of the world unloading annually at this artificial harbor, for the improvement of which 40,000,000 cubic yards of silt have been dredged from the river-bed. Manufactures are multiform and of large volume, especially those of iron-works and machine-shops; for here are controlled the metallurgical industries of Scotland. Commerce is in proportion, exports exceeding 1,500,000 tons a year, with coal and iron in various forms as the principal items. Glasgow is one of the best governed cities in Europe; its gas and water works, — the latter costing £2,500,000 — its street railroads, parks, squares, and sanitary arrangements being under the control of a corporation of practical business men. Among the finest buildings are the cathedral, the exchange, and the university; the last in the form of a quadrangle, 530 by 290 feet, the spire of its central tower rising 300 feet above ground.

GLASGOW

Its cost, including that of the handsome common hall erected by the marquis of Bute, was £500,000.

Edinburgh, situated on a cluster of hills separated by deep ravines and overlooking the broad estuary of the Forth, is as to site one of the most romantic of European cities; buildings in themselves without beauty of design blending happily with the surrounding scenery, which is here of surpassing loveliness. The castle, for several centuries the residence of Scottish monarchs, is probably the most ancient structure, and around it still cluster the steep, narrow streets and tall, quaint houses of the old town, destroyed

OLD EDINBURGH

by fire and rebuilt about the middle of the sixteenth century. In the new town, composed of massive and costly edifices, are many handsome thoroughfares, of which Princes street, with its public gardens where is the Scott monument, is one of the finest in the British isles. Connecting the two quarters is a huge embankment called the mound, at the foot of which are the national gallery and the royal institution, both of classic architecture, the former containing a choice assortment of paintings, and the latter a valuable collection of antiquities. Holyrood palace, built on the site of a twelfth century abbey, has also its picture gallery, where are the portraits of Scottish sovereigns, including that of the ill-fated queen of Scots, of whom a few relics are still preserved.

MARY, QUEEN OF SCOTS, JANETTE

In parliament house, where met the assemblies of the Scottish estates, and where now the supreme courts hold session, the architectural feature is the great hall with its handsome oaken roof. In another apartment is the advocates' library, with 300,000 volumes and many valuable manuscripts. Though originally a private collection, it is regarded as a national library, and is one of the few entitled by the copyright act to receive a copy of every work published in Great Britain. Among other libraries is that of the university, founded in 1582, and now containing some 4,000 students and a large corps of professors, whose quarters are in a massive quadrangular structure erected near the close of the eighteenth century. In connection with it are the botanical gardens and the observatory, one of the finest edifices on Calton hill. Edinburgh has long been noted as one of the foremost of capitals in literature, science, and art, though no longer deserving its former title of "the modern Athens," as in the days of Robertson, Adam Smith, and David Hume; of Jeffrey, Brougham, John Wilson, and Walter Scott. It has many churches, colleges, and charitable establishments, with scores of fine monuments; while of business buildings one of the finest is the bank of Scotland, an imposing renaissance structure.

ADAM SMITH

Connected with Edinburgh by continuous lines of streets is its port of Leith, a bustling place; and not far away is Dundee, also a thriving seaport, and from time immemorial famous for its linen manufactures. North of the latter is Aberdeen, one of the foremost of Scottish cities in population, industries, and wealth, and with much of historic interest; the first of its many charters being granted by William the Lion in 1179. It is a well built town, constructed mainly of granite and with many handsome edifices, among which is the university, occupying the site of a Franciscan convent. Its harbor, naturally defective, has been greatly improved within recent years; its docks are well lined with vessels, and from its shipbuilding yards have been launched some of the finest and fastest clippers that sail the seas. Among inland towns are Perth, the ancient capital of Scotland's kings; and Stirling, with its high-mounted castle, once their favorite residence. Inverness, the highland capital, though one of the oldest towns in northern Britain, wears a modern aspect, and in its suburbs are many beautiful villas. On an adjacent hill, where now are the court-house and jail, stood the castle mentioned by Shakespeare in his tragedy of Macbeth.

STIRLING CASTLE

On the bank of Dee and some fifty miles west of Aberdeen is Balmoral castle, the favorite summer residence of the queen, where in the company of her children and grandchildren she enjoys her holiday in simple fashion, amid the beautiful scenery and bracing air of the highlands. The estate was leased, and afterward purchased by the prince consort for the sum of £32,000; but many thousands of acres have since been added, together with a roomy and comfortable mansion erected by the prince in the baronial style of Scottish architecture.

BALMORAL

From the little Welsh port of Holyhead, in the isle of Anglesey, the swiftest and best appointed of channel steamers run to the harbor of Kingstown, whence a few miles' journey by rail brings us to the capital of Ireland. It is a beautiful town, with spacious thoroughfares, handsome buildings, and in its suburbs one of the finest parks in the world; but with little of the business stir that should characterize a city of metropolitan rank. The men of Dublin hold traffic in contempt, and would rather live amid the semi-starvation of poor and affected gentility, as members of the civil service, as military officers, or briefless barristers, than make their fortunes as tradesmen or even as merchants. Yet that all are not so silly is shown by a considerable volume of commerce, as appears from customs receipts of about £1,250,000 a year. Within recent years the docks on the Liffey have been greatly improved, the river deepened, new wharves erected, and a commodious basin completed; yet the total of all Dublin exports is less than £100,000 a year, while those of Belfast, with little more than two-thirds the population, are at least five times as much.

DUBLIN

Of many costly and imposing edifices the finest and largest is the bank of Ireland, formerly the parliament house, covering five acres of ground and requiring few alterations to adapt it to its present use. In front of the main facade, with its projecting wings, is a colonnade of the Ionic order; another colonnade in the form of a quadrant connecting it with the western front; while on the eastern side, where was the entrance to the chamber of the lords, is a row of Corinthian pillars. Trinity college, though a plainer structure, or rather group of structures, is of massive but symmetrical proportions. The interior of its chapel is beautifully decorated, and in its examination and dining halls are portraits of Edmund Burke, of Bishop Berkeley, of Grattan, Yelverton, Flood, and other famous Irishmen. The library of Trinity is the best in Dublin, though the one attached to St. Patrick's cathedral, founded in the twelfth century and since rebuilt in greater splendor, is richer in valuable manuscripts. The income of the college, mainly from rented estates, exceeds £70,000 a year; there is an average attendance of about 1,500 students, and its graduates include some of the foremost scholars of the age.

Among other institutions worthy of note are the royal college of science, with a parliamentary grant of £7,000 a year, though the number of students is seldom more than forty; the royal Dublin society with a grant of £7,500 for the maintenance of a library, museum, and art gallery; the national gallery with about £2,500, and the royal Irish academy, whose allowance is of similar amount. The reform club is one of the foremost of social organizations. The Four courts, erected at a cost of £200,000 on the site of a Dominican monastery, are the headquarters of the judiciary, while Dublin castle is the largest and by far the dingiest of all the great buildings, though with handsome tower and chapel. Monuments are plentiful in Dublin streets and pleasure grounds; that of Wellington, an obelisk 200 feet in height, standing in Phoenix park; among others in the city proper are those of Nelson, Grattan, Burke, Goldsmith, O'Connell, and Thomas Moore.

Belfast, on the northeastern coast, is the commercial metropolis of Ireland, and also her chief manufacturing city; its prosperity dating from near the middle of the seventeenth century, when Thomas Wentworth, the first lord-deputy, bestowed on it certain fiscal rights. At that date there were less than 1,000 inhabitants, dwelling in 150 houses, chiefly of mud and roofed with thatch; in 1395 the population was estimated at 275,000 and the buildings at nearly 40,000. In 1695 some 50 ships with a total burden of 4,000 tons sufficed for the carrying and export trade. In 1895 more than 10,000 ships with a total of 1,750,000 tons were entered inward, and there were at least as many clearances, exports probably amounting to £30,000,000. Linen, and especially linen yarns, is the principal branch of manufacture, cotton-spinning, which at one time was the leading industry, having fallen into decadence. There is little of historic or architectural interest in this flourishing Ulster town, where all are intent on money-making, though among buildings recently constructed are not a few of superior design and workmanship.

Londonderry ranks next to Belfast among the seaports and marts of commerce in northern Ireland. It is an ancient town, among its oldest buildings being a monastery erected about the year 546 on the spot where now stands the bishop's palace, while still almost intact are the solid ramparts, with their seven gates, constructed early in the seventeenth century at a cost of only £9,000. To the latter date, though with later additions, belongs the Episcopal cathedral, built at the expense of the city of London, in the later English style, a presentable structure, but inferior to the catholic cathedral in architectural design. Factories and shipbuilding yards are numerous; and a considerable source of wealth are the salmon fisheries of the Foyle, across which is an iron bridge 1,200 feet in length.

Limerick, the fourth as to traffic of Irish ports, and connected with an extensive system of inland navigation, is also noted for its bridges, spanning the broad stream of the Shannon, one of them, erected in 1827, costing £85,000. Its cathedral of St. Mary, founded in the twelfth century and rebuilt in the fifteenth, is a cruciform Gothic structure; and there is also a catholic cathedral of modern date. Galway was at one time a rival of Limerick, but not within recent years, though still with a moderate shipping and local trade.

LIMERICK

Almost side by side with handsome residences and shops of modern design are quaint old-fashioned buildings in the form of a square, with central courts and ponderous gates opening into the street. Cork and Waterford are the principal seaports of the south, the former ranking third among Irish cities in population, commerce, and wealth. Some 10,000,000 or 12,000,000 bushels of grain, with a large quantity of live-stock, butter, and other commodities are here unshipped, exported, or marketed every twelvemonth, while several thousand coasting and sea-going vessels enter its spacious harbor. There are many fine business buildings; but for residence purposes Queenstown, with its genial climate and picturesque location, is the choice of the wealthier classes. Less than fifty miles toward the north is Killarney, now a modernized town with spacious thoroughfares and commodious dwellings, as befits this favorite resort of tourists and sight-seers. As to the beauties of the adjacent lakes, bordered by verdure-clad hills rising almost from the water's edge, nothing need here be said. Near Lough Leane, studded with wooded islands, where are the ruins of Ross Castle and the sweet Innisfallen of Tom Moore, stand hoar and solemn the picturesque remains of Muckross abbey, erected by Franciscan monks about the middle of the twelfth century.

KILLARNEY

Adjacent, and belonging to the United Kingdom, are many islands and island groups, as the Orkney and Shetland isles, the isle of Man, the isle of Wight, and the Channel islands, the last belonging geographically to France, but politically to Great Britain. The isle of Wight, separated by a narrow strait from the county of Hampshire, of which it forms a part, is on account of its scenery and climate a place much frequented by health and holiday-seekers, without whose support the inhabitants could not exist: for while there is no lack of resources, there are no industries, except a little farming, fishing, and shipbuilding. In the summer months Cowes, Ryde, Ventnor, and other watering places are liberally patronized; but in winter the place is dead. Jersey, the largest of the Channel islands, has a moderate volume of commerce, and though raising good crops of grain and fruit is noted rather for the richness of its pastures and the breed of its cattle, kept mainly for dairy purposes. St Helier, with its inner and outer harbor protected by a fortress that cost £1,000,000, is the only important town, and here are the homes of many poor gentlefolk; for living is cheap, though the days are gone by when a spacious mansion can be had for £10 a year, and the annual expenses of a family are less than the monthly expenses of one in London.

SHETLAND ISLANDS

MISCELLANY. — The Phoenicians used to visit the Britons for tin and lead, found to-day on the coast of Cornwall. The savage peoples then inhabiting these isles had no coins, unless the metal rings they used for money could be so called. Their basket-boats they covered with skins, and they made swords of mixed copper and tin. Their druids, or priests, made them build great temples and altars, religion here as elsewhere having a key to conscience and the money chest. This was as Caesar saw them shortly before Christ.

In his *Faery Queen* Spencer gives the cave of Mammon as the abode of his god of wealth, who is first a miser, then a worker in metals, and finally god of all the world's treasures, and whose daughter is Ambition.

The wealth of the Rothschilds is estimated at $2,000,000,000; it has doubled within 20 years, at which rate, in 100 years more, it will be $64,000,000,000.

During the heroic period of the Rothschilds' operations, one of their brokers was Moses Montefiore, whose ancestors, like the Disraelis, had come to England when the doors had been opened for them by Cromwell. Marrying within the Rothschild circle, he won for himself a colossal fortune on the exchange, and then became the apostle for his people. He aided in the removal of Jewish disabilities, so that his nephew, Baron Lionel Rothschild, could sit in the British parliament. On behalf of his suffering brethren throughout the world he made journeys to Africa, to Asia, and to various parts of Europe, travelling in princely state, in coach and six, by special train on land and chartered ship at sea. Backed by the power of enormous wealth, prince, potentate, and people bowed

SIR M. MONTEFIORE

before him, as his hand scattered largess such as few sovereigns could indulge in. His hundredth birthday, the 24th of October 1884, was celebrated in the chief cities of the world.

Among wealthy Scotchmen was the shipbuilder William Henderson, whose estate at his decease in April 1895 was valued at $5,000,000. He was one of four brothers who established the Anchor line of steamships, and all of whom died within a period of two years, William being the last of the quartet. They began with a small capital, and as late as 1863 had only three vessels afloat; but receiving financial assistance, they had 36 steamers in their fleet in 1872, while hundreds of craft of all kinds were built for others under their superintendence. The two yachts named *Valkyrie* came from their yards at Glasgow, as also did the *Thistle*, the *Galatea*, the *Genesta*, and the *Britannia*, the last belonging to the prince of Wales, the only boat that defeated her American competitor.

Baron Hirsch's estate of $65,000,000 was scattered throughout the various capitals of Europe. His great delight was in associating with royal personages, and for their friendship he was willing to pay.

Miss Coutts, the banker's daughter, inherited from her grandfather, who founded the London house in 1768, the lady assuming management in 1822, upon the death of the grandfather at the age of 91 years. Among her many benevolent gifts were the Columbia market and the church of St. Stephen.

To Thomas Guy were given the names of miser and philanthropist, though he was neither, — a miser because be won a fortune gambling in South Sea bubble stocks; a philanthropist because he gave £238,292 for which he had no use to gratify his vanity in founding a hospital to bear his name.

BURDETT-COUTTS

Osborne and Balmoral are the private property of the queen, as are also 600 rented houses, markets, ferries and mines, estates in Yorkshire, Oxfordshire, and Berks, lands in Isle of Man, Scotland, and Ireland, besides revenues from forests and other sources. She has four yachts, one of which cost $500,000 to build and $65,000 a year to keep. There are royalty houses everywhere, public and private; as Buckingham, Windsor, Richmond, St. James, Kensington, Hampton, Kew, Pembroke, Bushby, Holyrood, Bagshot, Gloucester, Clarence, and the rest.

HOLYROOD

The income of the church of England is estimated at $50,000,000 a year, most of which is absorbed by the bishops and archbishops, some thirty of whom have salaries of $15,000 a year and upward, while the archbishop of Canterbury receives $75,000. The inferior clergy are miserably paid, $500 being a large stipend for a curate, and $300 or at most $350 an average stipend. A collier or brick-layer can earn more, and a skilled mechanic at least twice as much. How the managers for Christ can reconcile to their consciences such wholesale self-appropriation of church revenues is past the understanding of the uninitiated.

Great Britain has made foreign acquisitions, mainly during the nineteenth century, of one-third of the surface and one-fourth of the population of the globe, having of square miles in America, 3,500,000; in Asia and Africa, each 1,000,000; in Australasia, 2,500,000. Thus for every acre of British soil, Great Britain has nearly 100 acres abroad.

Notwithstanding her enormous possessions, the average of property held in Great Britain is less than $1,500 per capita, though even this is larger than in France or the United States, which rank next in point of wealth. There are probably not more than 500,000 persons whose incomes exceed $1,000 a year; but there are 2,000,000 to 2,500,000 with incomes of $500 to $1,000. The number of wealthy families, — say those having $25,000 a year or more — does not exceed 6,000 or 7,000. A man worth $100,000 is spoken of as rich in England; and among the middle classes $500 to $750 is considered a maying income. The poor are very poor, and especially in London, where absolute paupers are numbered by hundreds of thousands, and nearly one-fifth of all the families must live on $5 a week or less.

The amount of foreign stocks held in Great Britain is estimated at the enormous total of $3,819,035,000, and the interest receivable upon them is $145,000,000 per annum.

The following figures may be of interest by way of comparison between the three greatest cities of the world. London, with a population of somewhat over 5,000,000, has 700,000 houses, an area of 80,000 acres, and 1,500 miles of streets; Paris, with 2,600,000 people, has 100,000 houses, an area of 20,000 acres, and 650 miles of streets; New York, with 2,200,000 people, has 120,000 houses, an area of 25,000 acres, and 600 miles of streets. In London the average is only 7 inmates to each house, against 26 in Paris and 18 in New York. In water supply New York takes the lead, furnishing 200,000,000 gallons a day, against 180,000,000 gallons for London and 120,000,000 for Paris. While the New York fire department is better than in either of the other cities; losses by fire are larger in proportion to population, averaging $5,000,000 a year against $7,500,000 in London and less than $2,000,000 in Paris. The municipal expenses of London are $75,000,000, of Paris $70,000,000, and of New York $45,000,000; the cost of lighting London streets amounting to $3,000,000 a year, New York about $1,000,000, and Paris at least $3,600,000; for Paris is the best lighted city in the world. The park acreage of Paris, apart from the neighboring forests of Fontainebleau, is 130,000 acres, while London and its suburbs have 23,000 acres, and New York has its Central park of 840 acres in addition to some minor areas.

LONDON PAVILION

As to the commerce and industries of Great Britain and Ireland, sufficient has been said to afford a general idea of their character, scope, and extent, while to describe them in detail would be impossible within any reasonable limit of space. It remains only to be added that the fisheries of the United Kingdom are a

REDDIN' THE LINES

very considerable source of wealth, the total catch averaging 500,000 tons a year, valued at £9,000,000 or £10,000,000. The deep-sea and especially the herring fisheries of Scotland alone give employment directly or indirectly to 120,000 persons, the annual sales of cured herring exceeding £2,000,000.

Marine insurance, though dating as Suetonius relates from the first century of our era, was unknown in England until 1598, and life insurance until 1706. The government, in addition to its 10,000 or more postal savings banks, conducts a life insurance business for the benefit of the poorer classes, but meets with poor success notwithstanding its hold on public confidence, for private companies offer better inducements. Its 30 years' operations have resulted in a smaller actual business than is transacted by some private companies in a single year.

From Russia, Germany, and Scandinavia, Great Britain has been importing lumber to the extent of about $45,000,000 a year, and from other sources about as much, making the annual imports of forest products $90,000,000. The elm, lime, chestnut, and poplar were introduced into England by the Roman invaders, and forestry began there prior to the time of Edward IV.

Much of the business of diamond cutting has been removed from Amsterdam to London; for in England are mainly owned the diamond mines of South Africa, the largest in the world. It is doubtless a profitable industry, for the world's diamonds are worth more than all its other precious stones put together; while perfect rubies are worth more per carat than the finest diamonds, they are extremely rare. Among the more famous brilliants in the possession of Englishmen is the "Hope blue diamond," named after its purchaser who paid for it $90,000. It appears to have been brought from India by the French traveller Travernier in 1641, when it weighed 112 carats, since reduced by cutting more than one half; but its history is somewhat doubtful.

The Manchester, England, corporation has in its service nearly 7,000 men who receive wages, yearly, to the amount of $2,250,000.

The contents of the London Zoological gardens are valued at £70,000, which includes one item of about £22,000 for animals, and another of £16,000 for books. The expenses of the gardens, about £24,000 a year, are almost covered by gate and other receipts, whatever is lacking being contributed by fellows of the society.

On its great ordnance survey map, now almost completed, England has expended more than $20,000,000 and 20 years of time. It has about 110,000 sheets, and the scale varies from 10 feet to the mile for the larger cities to one-tenth of an inch per mile for remote and mountainous districts.

CHAPTER THE SEVENTEENTH

AFRICA

To be thought rich is as good as to be rich. — *Thackeray.*

The shortest way to riches is by contempt of riches. — *Seneca.*

If we are rich with the riches which we neither give nor enjoy, we are rich with the riches which are buried in the caverns of the earth. — *Vishnu Sama.*

Riches, perhaps, do not so often produce crimes as incite accusers. Want keeps pace with wealth. Wealth may be an excellent thing, for it means power, leisure, liberty. — *Johnson.*

Wealth is an imperious mistress; she requires the whole heart and life of man. Life is short; the sooner a man begins to enjoy his wealth the better. Wealth is not his that has it, but his that enjoys it. If you would he wealthy, think of saving as well as of getting. — *Laboulaye.*

Wealth created without spot or blemish is an honest man's peerage, and to be proud of it is his right. — *Beecher.*

Covetousness is ever attended with solicitude and anxiety. — *Franklin.*

We never desire earnestly what we desire in reason. Avarice, which often attends wealth, is a greater evil than any that is found in poverty. It. is more opposed to economy than to liberality. — *La Rochefoucauld.*

It is not a social passion. — *Hazlitt.*

It is a passion full of paradox. — *Colton.*

It grinds like an emery; it seldom flourishes save in the poorest soil; it is generally the last passion of those lives of which the first part bas been squandered in pleasure, and the second devoted to ambition; he that sinks under the fatigue of getting wealth lulls his age with the milder business of saving it. — *Fielding.*

The desire of riches does not proceed from a natural passion within us, but arises rather from vulgar, out-of-doors opinion of other people. — *Plutarch*

If you would abolish avarice, you must abolish the parent of it, luxury. — *Cicero.*

The eye of an avaricious man cannot he satisfied with wealth, any more than a well can be filled with dew. — *Saadi.*

MIDWAY in our survey of the world's wealth, we come to the Dark Continent, early known but late to be penetrated by Caucasians. Here we are met by the still unanswered questions, Whence the inhabitant, with his black skin and woolly hair? Is he a son of Noah, or an autochthon? And what makes his skin black and his hair woolly, a father's curse or a southern sun? We will not question the possession of a soul, gravely discussed within the century, but grant him one, with all the rights and privileges inherent in all of God's creatures, whether possessed of souls or not.

The history of the Africans is not without its lessons; but we are not always ready to accept, still less to apply the lessons of history. Our ethics are only partially sound, made up as they are of truth and falsity, reason and unreason, common sense and uncommon foolishness. Intellectual vision, never of the clearest, is rendered yet more obscure by opaque clouds of tradition and prejudice, and if unpalatable truths are made too plain, we close our eyes and wrap self-love in previous opinions. We do not like to admit how little we know of ourselves, or can ever know of others, or whence or what the agencies which have come into man's being to make him what he is. We are loath to accept the principle forced upon us that the ultimate right is might, that whatever is, omnipotent and inexorable power has so willed it, and therefore it must be, even though the weak unjustly go to the wall. What is right? we then ask, and straightway institute search for the difference between ancient infamies and our own, those to which we have tuned our tongue to give the proper name, and those which self-interest and superstition constrain us to call progress, improvement, the greatest good to the greatest number. Time, the illuminator, the conscience-tamer, and healer, permits us now occasions to tell the truth. Time was when he would be scorned or persecuted who should say that every foot of land civilization rests upon is stolen property, even that whereon are reared our churches and hospitals and institutions of learning; yet we are just as ready as ever, while denouncing theft in the abstract or when practised on ourselves, to steal all the land in the possession of weak and defenceless peoples which is worth the stealing.

But this is not all, nor by any means the worst of it. We used to steal men, but that form of theft we have abandoned. Why? Optimists and philanthropists say because the world is growing better and men more humane. Perhaps so. But why then do not men cease from stealing lands and killing those who attempt to defend them? It is difficult to establish the theory that human nature has changed, however manners may in some respects have become refined. A century or two ago men were wanted more than land: now land is more coveted than the enforced labor of men. Property primeval consisted not only in air and sunshine, but in lands and streams and vegetation, while gold was of no special value, and so-called precious stones were worth no more than other stones. But at a very early date it was ascertained that human beings, if caught, could be utilized by the catcher as bondsmen, and thus the infamous practice grew, and developed into such vast proportions as to make it appear that on the whole, while many had grown rich thereby, slavery did not pay. Then Christendom pronounced it immoral. But it has not yet become immoral for European nations to enter the lands of defenceless peoples, take forcible possession, and proclaim laws; and should any rise and do battle for home and country they are called rebels, and butchered, with heralded glory to the butchers, all in the name of progress and Civilization.

For the first score or two of centuries of our history, men spoke plainly, and acted openly, claiming the right to rob, kill, and enslave; but since the gods have all left Olympus we must needs serve the devil under the guise of Christian charity. After all, if it tends to lessen cruelty or iniquity in any form, it may be as well to foster those schools of moralists whose leaders are able so clearly to show the difference between the old African slave trade and the trade which to-day permits men to enter Africa with book in one hand and sword in the other, to seize the country, and upon the first plausible excuse which offers to kill off the inhabitants.

The continent of Africa is teeming with wealth, and the great powers of Europe are quarrelling over its seizure and partition. That this inevitable accompaniment of our nineteenth century civilization, which sooner or later is visited upon all savage countries, has been here so long delayed, was due to wars at home and the still incomplete extermination of native races in India and America. Slaves and ivory and gold and diamonds were, however, too glittering prizes for the cupidity of dominant races forever to resist, and soon the black man, like the red man, will have to surrender his home, and then the yellow man's turn will come, when the souls of China's millions will be converted to Christianity and their property transferred to our pockets.

The seizure of Africa by European powers was somewhat similar to the seizure of America 400 years ago. The possessions of the weaker races are taken by the stronger as a matter of course, and as by divine right. The entire continent of Africa, except the Sahara and the interior of Soudan, has been appropriated by European nations in tracts of millions of square miles, — Great Britain 2,500,000, France 3,000,000, Germany 825,000, Belgium 850,000, Portugal 900,000, Italy 600,000, Spain 250,000, Turkey, 840,000 — leaving unappropriated besides Sahara and the Soudan, Morocco, Liberia, and the Boer republics — only about 1,600,000 square miles. It appears to be the will of God that Europe should possess the world, and that the Hittites and Amorites, the Hivites and Jebusites of America and Africa, of India and peradventure of China should be smitten and utterly destroyed.

One reason why the interior of Africa has remained so long undisturbed by the march of civilization is the malarious nature of a large part of its border, — reputed at least to have a climate deadly to Europeans — this, and the jealousy manifested by the various nations holding possession of different parts of the coast uniting to protect other portions from the inroads of foreigners.

Speaking generally, as far as general remarks can apply to a continent so large and diversified as Africa, from the low coast belts of either ocean, covered with yellow grass and scattering palms interspersed with swamps and inhabited between the widely separated native villages by the leopard and hyena, the crocodile and hippopotamus, the country rises first into a low and then to a higher mountainous plateau covered with forests of thin stunted trees. In the northern interior, back of the Atlas mountains is the Great Sahara desert, and in the southern interior are lakes and rivers, mountains and plains filled with vegetable and mineral wealth, the riches of royalty and nobility being largely in wives and slaves.

NATIVE KRAAL

Early in the movements of the human race, intimations of which come to us from the twilight of mythology, the most ancient nations of the east, and later of the Phoenicians and others, planted colonies along the Mediterranean shore of Africa, and even on the

Atlantic seaboard. Lybia, the continent was called, which Herodotus says was circumnavigated by Phoenician ships furnished by Pharaoh Neko, king of Egypt. But the Asiatics who cruised around the Mediterranean coast of Africa 3,000 or 4,000 years ago were not disposed to penetrate far into the interior, even had they been able to do so, in the absence of any large river west of Egypt. Nor were there great and wealthy nations to conquer and despoil, while stretching almost across the continent was the broad expanse of the Sahara, where according to tradition were quickly burned to ashes those who dared venture therein.

Of the settlements made upon the northern seaboard, those of the Phoenicians are of the earliest authentic record, though how far they explored inland has not even yet been determined, some saying that their traders were on the Niger, others only on a branch of the Nile. With their camels the Arabs could cross the desert with some degree of safety, penetrating as far as the Senegal and Gambia, and planting colonies at Sofala, Mombas, Melinda, and other points. Voyages were made along the western coast, if indeed the continent was not then circumnavigated by the Egyptians and Phoenicians, notwithstanding their fear of the sea of Darkness beyond the pillars of Hercules. It was of the people of this coast that the story is told by Herodotus, so often repeated and applied to other nations, as to the method of traffic, strangers landing and quickly retiring after leaving articles on shore, whereupon the natives would appear and place beside them other articles that they were willing to give in exchange. It is certain that long before modern Europe had any other than the vaguest knowledge of the country, Mohammedans had made their way inland and formed settlements on the banks of the Niger, among which were Ghana, later known as Wangara, and Tokrur, somewhat to the eastward. In the Niam forests to the south the followers of the prophet kidnapped the natives and sold them to the slave merchants of Barbary and Egypt.

CAMELS, ARAB LIVE-STOCK MARKET

Upon the general awakening from the relapse into barbarism which followed the dissolution of the Roman empire, the African coast attracted the attention, first of Spain and then of Portugal. In 1393 one Almonaster visited the Canaries, and in 1405 the dominion of these islands was granted by the king of Castile to the Norman baron, Jehan de Betancourt, who explored the coast beyond Cape Bojador to the Rio d'Oro, where he gathered much gold and many captives. Portugal then came to the front, and while the armament assembled at Lisbon awaited its orders for the attack on Morocco, certain adventurous captains sailed along the coast to a point whence mariners had hitherto believed it impossible to return.

When in 1415 the Portuguese took Ceuta, a town on the African coast opposite Gibraltar, Prince Henry was told by Moorish prisoners that beyond the Sahara, beyond the fiery zone which the ancients had deemed it impossible to cross, was a populous country, rich in ivory and gold. The people there were very black of skin, with short hair crisped to the head, probably by reason of the heat, which was so intense that it boiled the surf on their shore. This Henry of Portugal, who was one of the world's great men, with intelligence far in advance of his time, and with no taste for the frivolities of his father's court, resolved to gather in some of these black men with their gold and ivory and woolly hair. He was not afraid of the traditional heat, — that is to say he did not fear it for his captains, — and he had seen the surf boil when it was cold. So he drew around him the braver and more intelligent men of the nation, and opening a school of navigation and discovery at Sagres, near Cape St. Vincent, sent forth expeditions which resulted in the occupation of the Gold coast by the Portuguese, and the opening up by sea of the negro slave trade. A gold mine was profitably worked at Approbi, and so great was the yield at another point, that the place took the name of Elmina, and a settlement was formed there, with fort, soldiers, and church, and all the appliances needed for entrapping and converting the natives. Thus while the illustrious Genoese was preparing to open a pathway for Europeans to the land of the naked red man in America, John II of Portugal was deriving his revenues largely from the robbery of the naked black man in Africa. Claims were subsequently preferred by the French to the ownership of the Gold coast, on the ground of discovery prior to that of the Portuguese. Villault was there in 1666, and found French names on the Grain coast, where settlements had been made by the Rouen Company about 1616, on the strength of which he claimed priority of possession for the French of the Gold and ivory coasts as well, but without success. Further than this, Prince Henry, in 1433, had obtained from Pope Eugene IV a bull granting to Portugal all lands which had been or might be discovered beyond Cape Bojador.

In 1486 was organized under the auspices of King John the Guinea company, two fleets thereafter making annual voyages between Lisbon and the Gold coast. Whenever the Africans attempted to defend their property or their rights, the Europeans would slaughter them without mercy, as has ever been the custom in such cases, and is so to this day. So long as papal anathemas were feared by the other nations of Europe, the Portuguese were but little molested in their monopoly of the bodies and souls of these millions of Africans; but in due time the Dutch and English appeared, hungry for share, and were soon deep in the African trade for ivory, gold, and slaves, bargaining and kidnapping, attended with constant fighting with the natives and with each other, the French and Portuguese joining in the fray. It was a sight indeed for high heaven to smile upon, the Christian nations of Europe thus snarling like hyenas over the African and his possessions, while easily reconciling the most infamous outrages with the tenets of their faith. The Dutch and English, by stirring up the natives against the French, Spanish, and Portuguese were soon in

IVORY STORE, MENDULA

the ascendant, the states-general of Holland planting settlements, and establishing Fort Nassau at Mori, but later transferring them to the Dutch West India Company. The occupation of the Gold coast by the Portuguese covered a period of 160 years, from 1482 to 1642, while the Dutch remained for 232 years.

In 1618 James I of England granted a charter to Sir Robert Rich and certain London merchants for a joint stock company trading to Guinea. A second charter was granted by Charles I in 1631 to Sir Richard Young, Sir Kenelm Digby and others, the traffic in slaves being their chief object, as the gold and ivory trade had by this time almost disappeared. Slaves had already been brought from the African coast by the Portuguese, and the Spaniards had their slave mart, the traffic being sanctioned by the pope in 1517, and increasing with such rapidity that by 1539 the sales of human beings reached 12,000 a year. Sir John Hawkins opened the barter for England in 1563. Forts were built and posts established on the African coast; buying and kidnapping began in earnest, and with every facility to "take niggers and carry them to foreign parts" at the lowest possible price. A third charter was bestowed in 1662 on the Company of Royal Adventurers of England trading to Africa, including among men of exalted rank the king's brother, James duke of York, who besides other contracts agreed to supply the British West Indies with 3,000 negro slaves annually. Another company of royal adventurers trading to Africa was organized in 1672 with a capital of £111,000, the king and the duke of York being among the members. The English built forts in addition to those they had already on the coast, thus greatly increasing their facilities for supplying the world with African products, chiefly in the form of slaves. More battles and butcheries followed, whenever the people raised objections to the stealing of their property or the kidnapping of those who were to be carried off to death or bondage. In 1698 the restrictions on the trade were removed, and English owners of plantations in America were permitted to obtain their slaves direct from Africa, paying to the government ten per cent of the value of the cargo. This act, on its expiration in 1712 was renewed by parliament.

ROBERT RICH

There was quite a choice as to quality in the human chattels exported from Africa. The occupation of the country was divided among many tribes or nations, the Denkeras and Ashantees being conspicuous in Guinea. When the natives were at war with each other, the slave business was good, for then the prisoners taken on either side were offered in the market; hence European buyers found it to their interest to foster enmity not only among the aborigines but against all rival purchasers. The English Gold coast brand was regarded with highest favor in the West Indies. These goods were called Koromantees, from Cormantine, the place where the English first obtained their supplies. They were of a nobler race, and while more difficult of control, displayed greater courage and endurance than others, and commanded in price £3 or £4 a head more at the plantations.

The trade was not without its tricks. Young men from fourteen to twenty years of age were most desirable, but the middle-aged were made to look young by shaving the head and anointing the body with palm-oil, the teeth in their decay being the greatest tell-tale. Exporters usually purchased their cargo from native dealers, kidnappers, and chiefs at war. The buyer first had his goods examined by a surgeon, and then branded by a red-hot silver instrument on the breast or shoulder. The men were then ironed in couples, and placed in dungeons until shipped. On board the vessel they were fed twice a day, and allowed on deck during fair weather, though still in irons. So long as the trade was legitimate, that is under protection of government, the slaves were fairly well treated if they remained quiet; for their owners had the same interest in keeping them alive and landing them in good condition as if they had been so many cattle; but when the traffic became illicit, requiring more secrecy and watchfulness, and also more subject to outbreaks, their sufferings were something horrible, so much so that many thousands killed themselves to escape their physical and mental agony. Then came the pirates from their former nests in the West Indies, now broken up by government cruisers, plundering, capturing, burning, adding if possible to the terrors of the scene. In 1750 parliament passed "an act for extending and improving the trade to Africa," and a fifth English company was created, called the African Company of Merchants, whereafter 10,000 slaves were carried annually to the West Indies from the Gold coast alone. Meanwhile with their chief town and fort at Cape coast, British influence on the Gold coast increased, until as in India the affairs of the natives and the manipulation of rulers were in their hands. The wars of the Ashantees and Fantees assumed greater proportions, which gave the English still further opportunity to place their own tools as kings, and thus make still more secure their foothold, not only as against the natives but against other European nations. The slave trade was in due time formally abolished by European governments, but nevertheless the traffic continued until a much later period.

In regard to the gold mines in this vicinity, after a lapse of two centuries they were reopened in the auriferous district of Wassaw, on the head waters of the Bonsa river, a tributary of the Ancobra. Notwithstanding the many malarious swamps thereabout, rendering the climate deadly for Europeans, several companies were formed in 1877 and afterward; first the African Gold Coast company, then the Swanzy, the Effuenta, and others, a French company, the Abosso, later commencing operations at the place of that name. The cost of transportation,

WEMMER GOLD MINE, JOHANNESBURG

however, about $150 a ton, prevented the working of the mines at a profit, whereupon still other companies were formed with coast harbors nearer the mines.

The continent has been explored by travellers ambitious for fame, many of whom lost their lives in consequence. Mungo Park in 1795 crossed from the Gambia to the Niger, which latter river he followed to Silla, returning home in 1797. In a second journey in 1805 he descended the Niger to its mouth, passing Timbuctoo, and being killed by the natives at Boussa. Later voyages and explorations I can but briefly mention. The journey of Mungo Park was followed by that of the Portuguese Lacerda, in 1798, from Mozambique to Cazembe, where he died. In 1796-8 Homemann set forth from Cairo and was never heard from after reaching Murzuk. Two Portuguese traders crossed the continent from Angola to the Zambese in 1802-6. Then there were the expeditions of Tuckey to the river Congo in 1816; Lyon and Richie from Tripoli to Murzuk in 1819; Denham, Clapperton, and Oudney from Tripoli across the desert to Lake Chad in 1822-3; and a score of others before 1857, when Hahn and Rath, Bastian, Du Chaillu, Barton, and Speke appeared upon the scene. Silva Porto and Livingstone crossed the continent in 1853-6, the latter being in the lake region in 1861. After this came Baker and a host of additional adventurers, winding up with Cameron, Stanley, Gordon, and the rest. The continent has been crossed many times by prospectors for gold from Cape Colony as far north as the Zambesi river, or even Mozambique and Zanzibar on one side and Lower Guinea on the other.

Nearly 3,000 years ago was planted on the coast of Africa the commercial city of Carthage, which was 100 years old before Rome was founded. For several centuries the history of Carthage is the history of northern Africa, Carthaginian domination extending during that period from the altars of the Philaeni to the pillars of Hercules, including as provinces the Balearic isles, Malta, and Sardinia, besides settlements in Gaul and Spain. A triple wall enclosed the city, whose harbors were artificial, the most conspicuous feature within the walls being the Byrsa citadel later occupied by the church of St. Louis.

The ground about Carthage and Tunis is historic, even though the history itself be dead. Long before Tyrian Dido built her city, the white walls of Tunis glistened in the sunshine. Some people fancy that four or five thousand years ago the Canaanites despoiled by Joshua found refuge here; others that the first settlers of Tunis were the Amalekites and Philistines of King David's time. Here is where Regulus defeated the Carthaginians; there is where the Vandals and Romans fought, and from this shore sailed Genseric for such parts as God should permit. Five millions of human beings were slaughtered on this coast within a period of twenty years, during the wars of Justinian. Then came the Saracens, and after them Louis IX of France; then Barbarossa, who taught piracy so effectually that the people practised it successfully for centuries; then Andrea Doria for Charles V captured Tunis and killed 30,000 of the inhabitants.

One of the greatest engineering works of ancient Africa was the aqueduct which supplied Carthage with 7,000,000 gallons of water a day. It was 40 miles in length, and mainly in the form of a series of stone arches. Near Susa, the amphitheatre of El Djem, or the Thysdrus as it was called, was regarded as the African colosseum, second only to that of Rome, being 430 feet in length by 370 wide, and with an arena 238 by 182 feet. In the games of its amphitheatres Africa copied Rome, and in the cruelty of its human sacrifices, Moloch, whose idol stood before the temple of Baal, need not blush before the demons of any religion created by man.

Tunis chiefly depended for future happiness on the mosque of Jami-al-Zeituna, which is likewise a college having a library where Islamism is taught.

CARTHAGE AND AQUEDUCT

In the European quarter are many modern built houses, mainly after the pattern of the French. The bey's palace contains some fine Moorish decorations in stucco arabesque. To repair the ancient aqueduct the bey, Mohammed-al-Sadik, expended $2,500,000. Now, as in the time of Leo Africanus, the leading manufactures are textiles, and especially silk-weaving, the latter dating from the coming of the Moors from Spain. Oils and essences, tobacco and leather are likewise here manipulated. While the bazaars of Tunis are fine, they are not equal to those of Constantinople and Cairo. As in all Moslem cities, traffic is arranged to save trouble for the purchaser by bringing together as many shops of a kind as possible. The centre of the oriental perfumery trade is here, and for this commodity alone is set apart an arcade 400 feet in length. Tripoli is a small Moorish city, with narrow, dirty, unpaved streets, and several mosques; it is the capital, forming with Benghazi, since 1835, a Turkish vilayet.

The Berbers, of what is now the French dependency of Tunis, are more Arabian than those of Algeria and Morocco. Their tribal self-government is democratic, their laws being different from those of the Koran; and they are a pastoral rather than an agricultural people, the pastoral nomads being almost as indolent and even more unruly than in the eleventh century, when first the country fell under Arab domination.

BAZAAR, TUNIS

The Barbary coast throughout its whole extent is well supplied with mineral wealth, iron and lead being the metals most widely distributed. Besides pine and deciduous oak, cork and zen trees cover large areas in Tunis, though the country is less wooded than in ancient times. Large grain crops are raised, notwithstanding imperfect cultivation; the olive and the vine are here conspicuous; in the uplands is esparto grass, and on the oases of Jerid the date palm. It was the grain fields and flocks, the oil and wine, the mines and fisheries of Tripoli, Tunis, Algeria, and Morocco that made Carthage great. Tripoli has some fertile land along the sea, the interior consisting of sandy plains and mountains which unite to form the Atlas range in Tunis. The figs, dates, and olives of Tripoli are of excellent quality, and prominent among articles of commerce and manufacture are pottery, castor-oil, ivory, and ostrich feathers.

OLIVE OIL MILL, KABYLE

In Algeria the Atlas range rises in places to a height of 7,000 feet, the Sahara side being a land of fruit and pastures, whose people are gardeners and shepherds, while the inhabitants of the fertile basins of the Mediterranean zone are largely grain-growers. The Berbers, the aborigines of the country, though inveterate thieves, are an active, industrious race, with villages in the higher elevations, and not without skill in the manufacture of guns, gunpowder, carpets, leather articles, and such agricultural implements as they use. There are also the turbulent Bedouins, or nomadic Arabs, who live largely in tents; the Moors, a mixture of races dwelling in villages near the coast; the Jews, money-lenders and merchants of the towns; also Turks, Kolougis, Negroes, and Mozabites; all these in addition to the Europeans, — French, Spaniards, Italians, English, Germans, and the rest.

Under Roman rule towns were built, roads made, and commerce and agriculture extended. But in the fifth century the Romans were expelled from Africa by the Vandals, who in turn were driven out by Belisarius, the Saracens acquiring the mastery in the seventh century, after which the country was divided into small states under petty chieftains, and straightway relapsed into barbarism. In the eleventh century arose the religious sect of Morabites, who founded the dynasty of the Almoravides, followed in the succeeding century by the Almohades, upon the downfall of whom the country was again broken up as before. Not content with driving the Moors from Spain, Ferdinand sent an army to Africa in 1505, and captured among other places Oran and Algiers. After this came the Turks, and then the Spaniards again, and finally France, and always the pirates, with whom the invaders were indeed one, as many of them were largely in the piracy business themselves, the most important point being on which side were the aggressors and on which the victims. Of late the country has become commercially very prosperous, discounts at the bank of Algeria doubling within a decade.

Even by the Romans Algeria was deemed a rich country, and is so regarded at this day, although the mineral deposits have never been fully developed, copper, lead, and iron being especially abundant. There is much fertile soil, five or six millions of acres being devoted to the raising of wheat and barley alone, while large areas are planted in cotton, flax, tobacco, and vineyards. Oran ships large quantities of esparto grass, used in the manufacture of paper. Algeria imports from France, Spain, Great Britain, and Italy $35,000,000 worth of cotton-goods, sugar, wines, salted fish, and other commodities, exporting live-stock, hides, wool, vegetables, tobacco, raw cotton, olive oil, flax, and ores, to the value of about $25,000,000.

ORAN

Before Algeria became a French province, and while in possession of the Turks, it comprised the four provinces of Algiers, Titterie, Tlemcen, and Constantine, the last three governed by beys, under the general rulership of the dey. It is now divided into the three departments of Algiers, Oran, and Constantine.

Morocco marks the western verge of ancient occupation. In area it is twice as large as Algeria, and five times larger than England. Though old in history, and bordering the highway of nations, there are portions of the country, as the Rif hills, which still remain unexplored by Europeans. The coast towns were founded by various nations, and destroyed and built again, Portugal, Spain, and Italy regarding it as rare sport to bombard the little towns along the Barbary coast on any slight pretext. Though averaging 4,000 or 5,000 feet in height, there are peaks in this west end of the Atlas chain rising from 10,000 to 13,000 feet above the ocean.

There are extensive mineral deposits in Morocco, — Jebel Hadid, or the iron mountain; copper and lead near Tetuan; antimony and gold in various places. Among the mountains are areas of woodland, though small as compared with the forest wealth of ancient times. As a rule the Moors will labor only to satisfy their requirements; and it is said that not more than one hundredth part of the agricultural land in Morocco is under cultivation. The camel is the animal drudge of the country, horses being used for war and personal service or display. There are horned cattle, sheep, and fowls in abundance. In the coast fisheries is a never failing source of wealth.

For beauty of situation the city of Morocco is unsurpassed, embowered as it is in groves and gardens between the mountains and the sea. It is surrounded by a dilapidated wall 30 feet high, with square towers 360 feet apart. The tower of the Kutubia mosque is the most conspicuous object; the houses are not high, and are for the most part built of clay; the sultan's palaces cover considerable ground, walled in, and with fine parks and gardens. The making of and working in red and yellow leather employs a large number of men. In place of its ancient population of 700,000, the city has now about 50,000 inhabitants.

Fez is a city of lofty minarets, stately domes, and flat-roofed houses, surrounded by a crumbling wall, but seated amid a plain of verdure streaked with silvery streams, gigantic aloes marking the paths which intersect the vast fields of grain. Founded in 808, before the end of the century, if we may credit the historian Kaldun, Fez rivalled Bagdad in wealth and splendor, and was called the Mecca of the west and the Athens of Africa. Chief among its numerous mosques were those of El Caruin and Edris. In the middle of the eleventh century Gregory IX founded here a bishopric. Under the Almoadi schools of science and philosophy were established, with a large library of Greek and Latin manuscripts, and hither came scholars and learned men from every quarter of the Levant. At that time the city, with its 86 gates and 30 suburbs, had great hospitals and baths, 10,000 shops, 90,000 houses, and 800 mosques. It now contains, among its 150,000 inhabitants, more than 8,000 Jews with their rabbis and synagogues, and stores of hidden gold. The women array themselves in gorgeous apparel, — red jacket and waistcoat covered with heavy gold braid and embroidery, green cloth petticoat trimmed with gold, flaming colored handkerchief covering the head, and red or blue silk sash round the waist.

ARAB SHOPS

Another holy Moslem city is Kairwan, some 80 miles from Tunis, which place it somewhat resembles, though by no means conspicuous for wealth or luxurious living. The mosque at Kairwan is not unlike a fort with minarets and stone towers. Within are 200 columns of marble, jasper, and porphyry, of Saracen Greek and Roman patterns.

Throughout the sultanate or empire of Morocco, rich men, both Jews and Mohammedans, make a practice of hiding their money, as a protection alike from government and banditti. Governors of provinces are frequently arrested by order of the sultan and thrown into the dungeon of Fez, there to remain with frequent bastinadoes until the hidden treasure is revealed. The city of Morocco, where are many goldsmiths and makers of enamelled pottery, exports wax, wool, and hides, and obtains from abroad European silks and trinkets. Tetuan makes inlaid damascened guns, and Mechinez and Fez swords of fine workmanship.

Mechinez boasts the most beautiful women in Morocco, and the finest gardens in Africa. It is said that in 1703 the imperial palace, founded by Muley Ismael, was two miles in circumference, and contained 4,000 women and 1,000 children. Near by was a great market, connected with the city by a road having on either side 50 fountains; also a grove of great olive trees, seven mosques, a garrison of artillery to hold in check the Berbers, and a government treasury containing $100,000,000. It was whispered in times past that within the palace was another palace, enclosed within three stone walls and lighted from above. It was entered by a low passage having three iron doors, and leading into a subterranean room where 300 slaves four times a year counted and packed up the gold and silver to be sent to the sultan, his imperial highness being present. The slaves were confined to this sepulchral treasure vault for life, never being permitted to behold the light of day. Around the great hall were standing ten earthen jars, which contained the heads of ten slaves who once tried to steal and escape, the operation which placed them there being performed by Muley Soliman.

ENTRANCE TO PALACE AND TREASURY

The Moslems hate Christians with bitter hatred, and have just cause to do so. When landing at Tangiers the passengers are brought ashore on the backs of Jews, of whom there are many here, both Spanish and Moorish. Christians are specially obnoxious to the mountaineers of the coast range, the Riffians of Morocco, and other Berber tribes, the Kabyles of Algeria, and the Tuaregs of the desert. All the tribes are fierce warriors, and the richest among them are those occupying the fertile valleys of the mountainous region, their possessions consisting chiefly of fine horses and many cattle. The nineteenth century was well advanced before this huge nest of pirates by sea and brigands by land was rooted out, Tangiers being bombarded by the French in 1844, though many years later both piracy and brigandage were practised as opportunity offered.

Tetuan was populated largely by refugees from Granada, when the Moors were driven from Spain by Ferdinand and Isabella. They were a people superior to others of their race, and their city displayed more refinement and luxury than those in its vicinity. The wealth they had they did not hide away, but employed it for the betterment of themselves and their neighbors. Tetuan is larger than Tangiers; the streets are wider, and the houses better built. Of the 22,000 inhabitants, 14,000 are Moors and 7,000 Jews, the greater part of the remainder being Spaniards. Business centres among the guilds, though the shops where diverse branches are conducted are open side by side.

TETUAN

Sahara, lying between the Barbary Coast and the Soudan, and extending from the Atlantic ocean through Africa and into Asia, is almost as large as Europe, although it has a population of less than 3,000,000, Arabs, Berbers, and negroes living in tents and brush huts, while Europe, where the mind as well as the body is nurtured and cultured, supports more than a hundred times that number in substantial structures. The surface one would hardly call diversified, notwithstanding the undulating sand-dunes of the west and north, and the mountains and plateaus of the south and east. There are several trade routes over which the commerce is considerable; as from Morocco to Cairo; from Kuka to Murzuk and Tripolis; from Tripolis to Soudan; from Timbuctoo to Tripolis; from Tunis and Algiers to Timbuctoo; from Timbuctoo to Morocco. The Sahara is by no means all desert; the northern part, though mountainous, has much fertile land of the date-growing quality, while the southern section, which borders on the great desert, is alternately sterile sand and oasis. The Sahara villages are engroved among fruit-trees, conspicuous among which, besides the date-palm, are the peach, apricot, fig, and pomegranate, and also the vine. In the mountains nearest the coast are forests of cedar, maple, ash, and other trees, some of them very large. Besides the several grains,

FRUIT MARKET, TRIPOLI

cotton, sugar, and tobacco are cultivated. In some parts of the 2,000 by 1,000 miles of sandy stretch, there is a temperature in the hottest days of summer of 150 degrees Fahrenheit, which is exceedingly severe on caravans where the wells are ten days' journey or more apart. Entire tribes have been known to perish where the wells have dried up, and no one but an acclimatized Moor, Berber, or Arab could live for a single summer day without water in the heart of the rainless district.

South of the Sahara, the Soudan, or country of the blacks, as the mediaeval Arabs named it, though likewise called Nigritia, or Negroland, has an area of 2,000,000 square miles, and a population, perhaps, of 80,000,000. In elevation it stands midway between the low-lying sands of the desert and the high plateau, varying from arid sterility on the north to fertilizing moisture in the south. The climate is tropical, with rains from April to October; redundant forest vegetation interspersed with prolific alluvial soil, and heat, dry or damp, everywhere. The plants most cultivated besides grain are cotton, tobacco, hemp, and indigo. Among the multitude of Soudanese animals the elephant stands first, and as a source of wealth, quite alone. Beasts of prey are innumerable, and here has ever been an unfailing source whence Asiatics and Europeans could draw their slaves.

The elephant is rapidly disappearing from Africa, and with the decline of the ivory trade the slave trade declines, as thousands of slaves were bought to carry the ivory to market. When the diamond and gold fields of the country have also been exhausted, it will be ready to turn its attention to something more valuable, and develop its real resources. At $2.50 a pound the tusks of an elephant are worth $150, while the elephant itself aside from its tusks is worth little or nothing. Slaves, ivory, diamonds, and gold are not the most solid foundations for wealth, and until these have disappeared, slight use will be made of the immense tracts of fertile land available for settlement.

In the dark continent, as elsewhere, fortune is fickle, debasing the proud and exalting those of low degree. Tripoli traders from Bornoo in the Soudan tell of one Rabah, a tall bony negro, recently a slave but now a ruler absolute, with an army at his back, having the latest and best repeating rifles, and a treasure-house filled with gold, silver, ivory, feathers, and coral. First as lieutenant under Zebehr Pasha, formerly Egyptian governor of Darfur, then as tax-collector in the Soudan, making his way with a band of fighting men to Baghirmir, southeast of Lake Chad, he not only worsted the Mahdists, but conquered the country, capturing Ashem, the Sultan of Bornoo and his capital, Kuka, on Lake Chad, and defeating Klari, Ashem's nephew, who attempted to succeed his uncle as sultan.

As in other savage lands, slavery has been common in Africa from the earliest times, but both the domestic and foreign slave-trade has been carried on throughout this continent as in no other part of the world. Perhaps it arose from Noah's curse of Canaan, and if so it comes hard on his innocent descendants; or it may be that the innumerable tribes and nations constantly at war with each other found it more profitable to enslave than to kill their captives. Then when the Mohammedans appeared as purchasers, and after them the Christians, kidnapping and slave-hunting became lucrative occupations.

In truth the African slave-trade may almost be termed indigenous; for it would appear to spring from the soil. Of three natives sent on a mission, two will often conspire against the third and sell him into slavery. Fathers sell their children, husbands their wives, and mothers their babes. Every year are brought into Morocco from the Soudan 3,000 slave boys and girls eight or ten years old, many of whom die of home-sickness. The ruling price is $6 for a boy and $12 for a girl, the government receiving five per cent on the value of the importation. As now conducted negro slavery in Morocco is of a mild and patriarchal character, the slaves being well treated, and for the most part not caring to be free. They prefer being provided for by a master rather than to assume the cares and responsibilities of life on their own account. In all the interior cities are market-places for the sale of slaves, but on the seaboard the traffic is conducted secretly, owing to European disapprobation; hence prices here range higher, say from $25 to $100, or sometimes even $200.

In equatorial Africa, as in Morocco, domestic slavery is a practice entirely distinct from the foreign slave trade. The former institution, where the slave remains among his friends and relatives, is kindly cared for, and relieved of the responsibility of providing for himself, is a very different thing from the traffic in human beings by the followers of Christ and Mohammed.

The three Africas, north, south, and central, are as distinct in history and character as Egypt and Palestine, or as Phoenicia and Spain. Of the great rivers of the continent, the Nile, the Zambesi, the Orange, Congo, and Niger, the course of the last two differs not greatly from the line of the equator. Of the lakes several assume the proportions of inland seas, as the Nyassa, 350 miles long; Tanganyika, 450 miles, and the Victoria and Albert, each with a surface of about 30,000 square miles. Inland commerce at the equator usually follows the courses of the rivers, not in a continuous stream as the water flows, but in stages and sections. For example, an inland tribe having slaves, ivory, ebony, india-rubber, or barwood to sell, cannot load its boats and descend the river to a white settlement, but must hand over its merchandise to the tribe below, to be passed on to the next, and so on, the last one selling the goods, retaining its commissions and passing on what is left to the one above, which thereupon takes its toll, until too often the amount that reaches the original shippers is little or nothing. This is a custom of long standing, and for a native to attempt to violate it means confiscation and slavery.

ROYAL PALACE, LAKE NYASSA

The staple food of the equatorial tribes is the manioc, besides which are yams, squashes, sugar-cane, and plantains. It is only in this region that the genuine negro is found, he of the coal-black skin and curly hair and protruding lips. The people of the southern and eastern interior, not to mention those of the northern seaboard or of the southern end of the continent, have not the form and features which characterize the dwellers in the slave-yielding lands of the Guinea coast and the river Niger, but rather a brown skin, with negro features wholly absent or but slightly pronounced. The wealth of the equatorial native consists less in what he has than in what he does not want; nature cares for him, and all nature is his; with that he is content. Usually buried with the dead African, as constituting his entire property, are pipe, knife, bowl, and bow. The black highlander grows a kind of millet, which constitutes his food, and of clothing he has none.

The Gold Coast, in Upper Guinea, was so called from the yellow metal found there, first probably by the Phoenicians, but certainly by the Dutch and Portuguese, the latter building a fort at Axim to protect the trade. Upon the later reopening of the mines there were unmistakable evidences of ancient workings by people other than natives. Deep tunnels, in one of which was an antique bronze lamp, were discovered, while primitive peoples never dig far for anything. Though not yielding as in former days, and with a hot climate unhealthy to foreigners, the Gold coast is still largely auriferous throughout its entire extent. Besides this the rich alluvial soil responds readily to cultivation, sending forth in abundance fruits and vegetables of all kinds, while the forests abound with merchantable timber. Here are found the egg-plant, the kola nut, the betel nut, besides ginger, indigo, the pineapple, and scores of other products.

Back from the seaboard of the Gold coast is Ashantee, a vast expanse of forest land where is still much gold left. Grain, fruit, and vegetables become prolific when put into the deep rich soil, and there is some manufacturing in the way of cotton cloth, pottery, and articles in gold and silver. It is a great thing to be monarch of Ashantee, with 3,333 wives and power to cut off heads at pleasure, better than to be king of England with only one wife and no power at all. On the other hand the nobility are not so independent as the nobles of England, though some of them have 1,000 slaves and bushels of gold; for if the king covets aught belonging to a subject, he has but to cut off his head and take it. Any noble who conducts himself circumspectly is permitted once during the year to show his wealth in the streets of Coomassie, greatly to the admiration of the beholders. Care is taken, however, not to display too much unwrought gold, as that falls to royalty on the death of the

GRANARY

possessor, and if the noble has much of it, and the king greatly needs it, the owner is liable to sudden death.

Yet more autocratic than his majesty of Ashantee is the king of Dahomey, doubly a king, for to his absolute temporal power is united the spiritual. The latter country derives quite a revenue from the duties on exported palm-oil and ivory, and on all imported articles. The king drives quite a thrifty trade in black maidens, daughters of the nobility and gentry, sent to him as gifts from their parents, and sold to his head men at good round prices, which immediately find their way into the royal pocket.

The negro republic of Liberia, established in 1822 by American philanthropists, was declared independent in 1847, and as such was later recognized by the leading powers of the world. The climate is hot and the soil rich, all the tropical products being easily grown on the low-lying coast; while the hills of the interior are suitable for cattle-raising. Metals are plentiful, though the mines are little worked. Some 18,000 descendants of slaves in the United States were here joined by 1,000,000 natives, and the result was not very flattering. The free black voters of the United States are better content with their political and social privileges in America than they fancy they would be with anything Africa can offer, preferring to sit in judgment over their former masters rather than display their talents in the land of their ancestors.

Congo Free State, with its 802,000 square miles of area, or four times the size of France, lies on the equator, and with its great navigable river as a central feature. Among the products ivory and india-rubber lead; then follow cotton, growing wild, coffee, the sugar-cane, resinous and copal gums, palm-oil, piassava, cocoa, pepper, and tobacco. For timber there are mahogany, ebony, rosewood, and teak, and for metals an abundance of copper and iron, as yet almost untouched, probably because the climate is dangerous to Europeans.

Senegambia, mountainous in places, with a low-lying coast on the north and marshlands with rank vegetation between, contains gold and other metals in abundance, and large tracts of rich alluvial land. Animals and plants, of which there are many varieties, are large and prolific, among the former being the wild-boar, lion, and leopard, and among the latter the baobab, accacia, and palm. In the Niger and Senegal swarm crocodiles and their associates, while the trees are filled with chimpanzees and others of the monkey and ape fraternity. The country is occupied by some 10,000,000 Moors and negroes, divided into numberless tribes, who fight and steal and live on the good things the gods provide. Foreigners here obtain gold, gums, groundnuts, india-rubber, oil, hides, feathers, ivory, wax, coffee, rice, and other products.

Loango has on its seaboard a fine primeval forest interspersed with mangrove swamps, grass prairies, and a tangled undergrowth of tropical vegetation around open parks and lagoons. Here are fragrant jasmines, thickets of lianas, a kind of olive myrtle tree, ipomoeas, and for native fruits the mango and papaw, while ginger and negro-pepper likewise grow wild. The staple food of the natives is manioc, though bananas are also a favorite article of food, while ground-nuts and tobacco are freely cultivated. There are, besides the chimpanzee and gorilla, seven kinds of apes, many birds of gay plumage, and snakes of many varieties. Until a recent period there was a large traffic in slaves, india-rubber and palm-oil being now the chief commodities.

Benguela has a mountainous interior with mines of silver, copper, iron, and salt, and an abundance of animal and vegetable life. Angola, back of its border of barren sandy plain, has tropical wealth of every variety, mineral, animal, and vegetable, conspicuous among which since the decline of the slave trade are gum, wax, and ivory.

Congo has copper mines at Bembe which were early worked by the Portuguese. Malachite is also found, and in the north, iron. Then there has been reported a lake of bitumen, and in several places are garnets, rubies, and the gum-copal, which is used as a varnish. Among the flora the oil-palm is conspicuous, also on the coast is the cashew tree, while cassava, ground-nuts, yams, and maize are cultivated in various districts. The king of Congo is a sorry looking monarch, his palace being a hut of reeds, while his nobility and gentry, unable to pay a Bond Street tailor, or obtain credit, must needs go naked.

Calibar has an alluvial soil covered with bush except the small portion which is under cultivation and the rocky interior. Here are for sale bamboo, maize, plantains, sugar, pepper, yams, and ebony and other woods.

Sierra Leone produces ginger, pepper, kola nuts, and cassava, besides coffee, cocoa, and corn. The rainfall of 160 inches is precipitated during nine months of the year. On the river Gambia are several factories, or trading posts, whence come wax, hides, gold-dust, ivory, palm-oil, gum-arabic, ground-nuts, and honey, though shipments are small considering the resources of the country.

During the first half of the present century a marked aversion to the presence of free colored persons existed in nearly all the states of the union, and some of them passed laws for their expulsion. It was thought by many that the best thing for the free negroes in the United States would be to settle them in colonies on the coast of Africa. In 1815 Paul Cuffee, a wealthy and patriotic colored man, sea captain, of New Bedford, Massachusetts, sailing his own ship, carried thirty-eight passengers mostly at his own cost, to Sierra Leon, and the year following was formed the American Colonization society under whose auspices some 5,000 persons were sent to Liberia, their town being named Monrovia, in honor of James Monroe.

Ancient Ethiopia was renowned for culture and advancement when Greece and Rome were at their best. Now the Ethiopians are widely scattered, being conspicuous in the region round the sources of the Nile, in Abyssinia, and Nubia, where are still to be seen remains of their former civilization.

Abyssinia is a mountainous plateau, with metamorphic rock of a metalliferous nature as a base. The climate is delightful, and the soil fertile. Among its streams are the tributaries of the Nile, recuperated by the periodic rains falling from June till September. Almost anything can be grown, three crops sometimes being raised during the year. Coffee is indigenous, and also many fruits. Conspicuous among land animals are the rhinoceros, buffalo, lion, and leopard, and in the rivers hippopotami and crocodiles. The *Koran* tells the story of Solomon and the queen of Sheba, who came at his bidding from Ethiopia, or Abyssinia, and presented him, among other things, with a son who was named Melech. The king summoned all the birds to appear before him; but the lapwing did not come, whereat the monarch was wroth and ordered the bird to be killed. But presently the lapwing appeared before the king and said, "I come from Saba, a queen reigning in great magnificence; she and her subjects worship the sun." Then Solomon sent by the lapwing a letter to Saba, ordering her to come at once and submit herself to him, and accept the true religion. And she came, bringing 500 men slaves and 500 women slaves, 500 bricks of solid gold, a crown, and many other presents, and submitted herself to Solomon and his religion.

The Somali, Mohammedans of Arab descent, in places settled and elsewhere nomadic according to occupation, grow crops of various kinds, raise camels, goats, and fat-tailed sheep, and collect frankincense, myrrh, and other gums, which together with other native products are exported to Arabia and India. Commerce is

BASKET MARKET

almost entirely in the hands of Hindoo traders, who almost from time immemorial have been settled on various portions of the coast.

In the sultanate of Zanzibar is a soil which will readily produce two grain crops a year, and four of manioc, the staple food. Here also flourish the clove, cocoa-nut, nutmeg, cinnamon, and other trees. The island seems to rest on coralline reefs, and the ancient forests have to a great extent disappeared. The island of Pemba is held by Arabs in large plantations worked by slaves. The Swahili coast is low-lying and swampy, the dense tropical vegetation under a heavy rainfall and hot sun breathing a pestilential air. Here are found the copal-tree and other economic plants, the land being especially adapted to sugar, cotton, coffee, and spices. The city of Zanzibar, the next largest to Alexandria and Tunis on the north and east African coasts, is divided into two districts, one called Shangani, devoted to commerce, government, and the palaces of the sultan, the other the poor quarter occupied by porters, fishermen, and slaves. The imports, largely of cotton cloth and other European articles, reach $6,000,000 as against $1,000,000 in exports of ivory, caoutchouc, sesame seed, and cloves.

From Zanzibar the Arabs carry on a large trade with the interior in ivory and slaves. Over a wide area are planted their encampments, communication with which is kept up at intervals by caravans, well armed and supplied with articles with which to purchase ivory and the slaves to carry it. Between the arrivals of caravans at the several posts the ivory is bought up and collected, and the captives made during the tribal wars, in addition to those who are stolen, furnish the slaves.

The coasts of Somali and Zanzibar are rich in traditions as well as in things material. Here, as in Abyssinia, was one of the many alleged residences of the queen of Sheba, and at Seychelee it is related that Adam and Eve took up their abode after retiring from Eden. At Mombasa stands the fort built by Vasco da Gama in the sixteenth century. Date and cocoanut plantations are now conspicuous. The reception room of the sultan of Zanzibar glitters with crystal chandeliers, while the walls are hung with red panels bearing quotations from the *Koran* in gilt letters, and the floor is covered with a thick crimson velvet carpet on which inlaid tables and gilt sofas and chairs with velvet cushions are disposed. In the sultan's harem are 150 women, loaded with costly drapery and jewels.

Chiefs of the petty provinces of the interior delight in playing the part of sultan, having learned the role by contact with the Arabs. They have their royal huts, their black harems, and hiding places for their treasures, and bluster and fight each other as men both white and black have ever done. Besides slaves and ivory, the natives here count among their valuables cattle, and metals wrought in forms of weapons and ornaments.

The Portuguese colony of Mozambique takes its name from a small coral island on which stands the provincial capital. There are other islands which export calumba root, sesame, ivory, wax, and oil-seeds, turtle-fishing being profitable in some places. On the Zambesi river are several settlements, and a native fair is held annually at Zumbo.

Sofala is a land of gold and ivory and apes. Here is yet another Hiram of Tyre and queen of Sheba country, while as with many other places, certain persons have fancied this to be the Ophir of Solomon. In 1587 a Dominican monk, Joas Dos Santos, set forth for Mozambique and Sofala, spending eleven years among the Portuguese settlements of those regions. In 1609 he published a work entitled *Eastern Ethiopia*, in which he writes: "The merchandise from Tete goes down to Sene with the gold which is brought from the market of Massapa, in the kingdom of Monomotapa, where a large quantity is always to be met with, as the great and lofty mountain Fura (or Afura) is close by. Upon this mountain are to he seen the ruins of buildings constructed of stone and lime — a thing which is not to be found in the whole of the Kafir country, where even the houses of the king are only built of wood and earth, and thatched with straw. An old tradition current in this country affirms that these ruins are the remains of the storehouses of the queen of Sheba; further, that this princess got all her gold from these mountains, and that this gold was carried down the river Cuama (Zambesi) to the Ethiopian ocean, and taken thence through the Red sea to the coasts of Ethiopia above Egypt, where this queen dwelt. Others believe that Solomon had these magazines built, and that here was obtained that gold of Ophir with which his navies were laden; that between Afura and Ophir there is no great difference. It is quite certain that around this mountain range much and very fine gold is found, easily conveyed by means of this river, as is still done by the Portuguese, and was done before them by the Moors of Mozambique and Kilwa; and further, that as in those days gold is carried to India, so in former days it might easily have been taken through the Red sea to Ezion-Geber, and thence to Jerusalem."

The mountainous interior of Madagascar is bordered by forests, and contains many fertile valleys and plains where rice is raised. Iron and copper are the principal metals; there are also antimony, rock-salt, and plumbago. The flora of the island shows over 3,000 varieties of flowering trees and plants. Nearly all the fruits thrive well and many are indigenous' the inhabitants, collectively called Malagasy, are of Malayo-Polynesian stock, neither savage nor yet civilized. They follow agriculture after primitive methods, rice being their staple food. A long-handled shovel does the work of oxen and plough, and threshing is performed by beating the bundles of rice upon upright stones. Society consists of three classes, the andriana, or nobles; the hova, or freemen; and the andevo, or slaves. High priest as well as ruler is the king, whose palace is in Antananarivo, the capital, where rush houses are gradually giving place to structures of adobe and stone. The royal mansion and government buildings occupy the hill round which the city is built.

KING OF MADAGASCAR AND HIS SONS

South Africa was originally occupied by some of the lowest types of humanity, Bushmen, Hottentots, and Bantu; nevertheless they were a happy and contented people, with satisfied corporeal wants and living in close communion with nature, while among civilized nations it would be hard to find more practical philosophy, or a nearer solution of the great problem of life, — liberty and the pursuit of happiness. In Zululand are many gods, one among whom is the creator of all and above all. These deities are responsible for everything that happens; nothing is left to chance; by proper attention to signs and omens they may know what the gods would have them do. The spirits of their ancestors afford them lesser gods, while to the supreme being they offer propitiatory sacrifice. Among their shrewdest and most able men are the wizard, or

NATIVE MEDICINE MAN

witch doctor, the rain-maker, the lightning controller, the ruler of the hail and other like professionals who live and acquire wealth on the credulity of their fellows. They do not in every instance claim supernatural powers for themselves, but act as mediators between gods and men. Every ill as well as every good comes from some deity, but one who may perhaps have been influenced by friend or foe; sickness and death are always the work of an enemy.

The term South Africa includes Cape Colony, Natal, Orange Free State, and Transvaal, or the South African Republic. On the eastern side of this southern extremity of the continent are Gazaland. Sofala, Mozambique, and Zanguebar; on the west Benguela and Guinea; in the interior Bechuanaland and Congo Free State, and stretching far away to the north the Great Desert. Traces of occupation by a people superior to the present aborigines are found between the Zambesi and Limpopo rivers. Except on the seaboard, where there is some malaria in places, the air is dry and healthy. The cool season is from May to November; a hot, moist, and enervating atmosphere prevails during the remaining months. A mean temperature of from 60° to 70° extends over large areas, rising above or falling below this at various points. The average annual rainfall at Grahamstown is 32 inches; Pietermaritzburg 30 inches; Capetown 23 inches; Graaff Reinet 13 inches; Worcester 11, Mossel Bay 12 inches; Simonstown 27 inches.

Before the coming of the Europeans South Africa swarmed with game, the lion, leopard, elephant, rhinoceros, hippopotamus, giraffe, zebra, antelope, buffalo, and many others of strange form and name being common. Then there are the hyena, wolf, wild dog, wild hog, baboon, and of birds, the partridge, pheasant, guinea-fowl, ostrich, and bustard.

On the coasts of South Africa are grown sugar-cane, tobacco, rice, coffee, and vegetables of many kinds, and in the interior flourish all the grains known to civilization, the uplands being devoted to grazing. The vine is prolific, the average yield in the best Cape districts being 380 gallons of wine to 1,000 vines. Land and labor are cheap, and irrigation encouraged by the several governments. Forests are few and good timber scarce. Mining, the most prominent industry, is mainly in the hands of large companies, the diamond fields of Kimberley being the largest in the world, while there are gold and silver

DE BEERS DIAMOND MINES, KIMBERLEY

in the Transvaal, and copper in Namaqualand. For seventy miles along the Vaal river 1,000 diamond-diggers gather stones to the value of £50,000 a year. Coal is plentiful on the upper plains, in the Stormberg mountains, and on the Zambesi.

Vasco da Gama was on the Natal coast on Christmas day, 1497; the Dutch were there in 1595; and in 1620 appeared the English. A Dutch settlement was established at Table Bay by 100 Hollanders under Jan van Riebeeck in 1651; trade with the Hottentots was opened; grain, fruits, and the vine were introduced from northern lands; mining was attempted but without important results; success in agriculture was more pronounced. The rule of Van Riebeeck was followed by that of other Dutch commanders and governors, and in 1685 Huguenots settled in Drakenstein and French Hoek. Permanent British occupation began in 1806 after wars with Holland and France, and the inevitable slaughter of the aborigines was inaugurated by the first Kafir war, as it was called, in 1811, at the end of which it is needless to add the English found their territory greatly extended. A second Kafir war in 1819, and a third in 1835, gave the English all they desired at that time of South Africa. Slavery was abolished in 1834, about one third of the value of the 35,000 slaves then in the colony being nominally allowed to the owners, but the greater part of it found its way into the pockets of government agents. So disgusted were the farmers, especially the Dutch Boers, with British rule, that more than 10,000 of them abandoned their possessions and crossed the Orange river.

Cape Town became the metropolis, with a population in 1895, including its suburbs, of more than 100,000. It is a handsome city occupying a beautiful site at the head of Table bay, and near the foot of Table mountain, the old-fashioned houses formerly clustered under shelter of the fort which Van Riebeeck erected in 1652, being replaced by buildings of modern design. It is well paved, well lighted, with a plentiful supply of water, and with all the appendages of a city of metropolitan rank. There are hotels, newspapers, street-cars, post and telegraph offices, churches, hospital, government buildings, railway, and breakwater. There are also the public library, university, and botanical gardens. The houses of museum, a government house, and parliament were completed in 1886 at a cost of £220,000.

PARLIAMENT HOUSE, CAPETOWN

The breeding of Spanish merino sheep was begun in Bredasdorp by J. F. Reitz in 1812, and in the mountains not far distant were raised horses and mules of excellent stock. Beaufort West has many fine sheep-walks, and the lands around Port Elizabeth, besides containing minerals, are of the best quality both for cultivation and pasture. Grahamstown is a pretty place, surrounded by a fertile country. The manufactories of South Africa are numerous but not large; wages are good, varying from the equivalent of $1.25 a day for laborers to as much as $3 or $4 for miners and mechanics, farm labor being mainly performed by natives, who receive From $2 to $4 a month with rations. In 1854 an epidemic, arising from night malaria, carried off 70,000 horses, thus seriously crippling an important industry. Ostrich farming is a prominent and fairly profitable occupation.

Durban the seaport, and Pietermaritzburg the capital of Natal, with populations of somewhat less than 30,000 and 20,000 respectively, are similar in most respects to other colonial towns of English origin. Each has its town-hall, costing about £40,000, besides markets, hospitals, churches, and other buildings of a public character. The people of Pietermaritzburg are justly proud of their park and botanical garden, the latter costing £60,000. The revenue and expenditure of Natal are about £1,000,000 per annum; imports £2,000,000 and exports £1,000,000. A considerable portion of the imports, however, are for adjacent colonies.

In establishing themselves at Natal, the English deemed it better to conciliate the powerful Zulu chief, Chaka, than to fight him. By means of gifts and a pacific attitude, they obtained permission to settle at Durban in 1823. Then followed the usual aggressions that attend the so-called progress of civilization and christianity in these distant lands. At the close of the Zulu and Transvaal wars the native warriors were few in number and shattered in strength.

Natal is rich in fertile soils and verdant landscapes. Rising in terraces from the seaboard to a grass-covered plateau 4,000 feet high, well watered by streams and possessing coal and other minerals in abundance, it is a land of almost limitless possibilities. The colony exports annually gold to the value of £250,000, Cape Colony £7,500,000, and Transvaal £3,500,000. Witwatersrandt, the most promising of all the Transvaal gold districts, is an undulating plain, 6,000 feet above sea level. The principal discoveries were made between 1854 and 1885, at which latter date the government declared nine farms adjacent to be portions of the public gold-field, whereupon the district was rushed by diggers.

NATIVE MINERS, SOUTH AFRICAN GOLD FIELDS

The Orange Free State, 4,000 to 5,000 feet above ocean's level, is mainly a stock-raising country, the chief town being Bloemfontein. The Great Karroo plateau is between the Orange and Molopo rivers, and of this the continuation is Bechuanaland. Mashonaland, in the Chartered Company's territory, is a gold-yielding district, and though hardly to be compared with Witwatersrandt, is honeycombed with ancient workings. North of the Zambesi the soil is fertile; the Milangi plateau has an annual rainfall of from 60 to 70 inches.

The Orange country has for basis of wealth abundant agricultural, mineral, and pastoral resources. The surface consists for the most part of a series of undulating treeless plains 4,000 or 5,000 feet above the sea, sloping northward to the river Vaal and southward to the Orange river, across which are the diamond fields of Kimberley and Griqualand West. Coal is here utilized and in the drift deposits along the river-beds are found pebbles of value and precious stones. Where once were the elephant, lion, rhinoceros, and giraffe are now sheep, goats, horses, cattle, and ostriches.

Mainly on account of the hatred entertained for the English was founded and built up by the Hollanders the Transvaal republic, Andries Pretorius, in 1848, placing himself at the head of the emigrant Boers then in the country, among the later presidents being Burgers and Kruger. The Lydenburg gold mines in the north, and the diamond developments in the south, directed attention to the country, stimulated railway building, and the growth of towns, especially that of Pretoria, the capital, which has its government house and other imposing structures, as the raadzaal, or parliament house, a fine building for an African colony, costing £138,000. To the national bank in the same vicinity is attached the state mint. There are scores of smaller towns, mining and agricultural, of which it is not necessary here to speak.

Transvaal, or the South African republic, is a platter-shaped plateau, for the most part with a dry invigorating atmosphere, and richer in mineral than in agricultural resources. Here are nearly all the metals in abundance, precious or otherwise, besides diamonds and other beautiful stones, these vast and undeveloped treasures being found embedded in porphyry, quartz, clay slates, and conglomerates. There are some forests, and much bush and grass land, stock-raising being the chief occupation of the Boers settled hereabout. Yet in some places two annual crops can be raised, and elsewhere tobacco, semi-tropical fruits, and the vine thrive well. Among native animals are the elephant, giraffe, zebra, rhinoceros, and others, all of which are gradually giving place to beasts of northern domestication.

MORNING MARKET, PORT ELIZABETH

To the Transvaal gold-fields Johannesburg, with a population in 1895 of something less than 50,000, owes its rapid growth and lively traffic. Sheep and cattle-raising were the main objects that brought men to these parts, and when gold was found in 1854, the government would not allow prospecting, lest the influx of foreigners should disturb the healthier industries. The restriction was removed, however, and in 1872 a reward was offered for the discovery of new and profitable fields. In 1886 the Sheba mine was opened and brought into the district 10,000 miners. Then was started the town of Barberton, and hundreds of wild schemes and limited liability companies were floated. The output of gold for 1894 was about 2,000,000 ounces.

The diamond fields of South Africa are at Griqualand West, near the southern extremity of the continent, and about equidistant from the east and west coasts and Port Elizabeth, which is on the same parallel as Cape-town, and about the same as Adelaide, Australia, on the one side, and Montevideo, South America, on the other, namely, south latitude 34°. The many small original claims have been consolidated into four principal mines, the Kimberley, Dutoitspan, De Beers, and Bultfontein. In order to meet the demands of all comers, the ground was at first cut up into strips of 31 feet square, for which a monthly license of ten shillings was paid, some of these little patches

FROM THE MINES

selling within a few weeks for £100 apiece, and within a few years for £10,000 or £15,000. The four mines were later controlled by two companies, employing several thousand miners, superintendents, clerks, brokers, and storekeepers.

In 1854 the country was nominally held by the Orange river sovereignty, and occupied by the followers of a Griqua chief named Waterboer. Later the sovereignty became a Dutch republic, and the country being open, bleak, and inhospitable, little attention was given to it, until in 1867 John O'Reilly, a travelling trader, saw at the house of a Boer named Niekerk a stone which attracted his attention. It was among some pebbles with which Niekerk's boy was playing. O'Reilly proposed to have it tested, and should he sell it, to return to the owner half the proceeds, which was done, the governor, Sir Philip Wodehouse becoming the purchaser at £500. Great was the excitement which followed, and soon the country was alive with prospectors and diggers, joint stock companies being formed at Cape Colony and Natal to search for diamonds in Griqualand West and especially on the Vaal river. A diamond was found in the plaster of a farmhouse at Dutoitspan, and the stone which led to the discovery of the Kimberley mine was picked up by a young man named Rawstorne, in the same vicinity. Another large brilliant, purchased in 1869 by a Dutchman from a Griqua native for £400 in goods, was sold soon afterward for £10,000. It was called the Star of South Africa, and has since been valued at £25,000.

A dispute arose between Waterboer and the Free State as to the ownership of the diamond fields, which were all within an area of three or four miles. Thereupon the British government stepped in, obtaining in 1871 a cession from Waterboer of his rights, and in 1876 paying the Free State £90,000 for its claim. Then set in an era of diamond mining in South Africa which virtually put an end to the industry in Brazil, just as the Brazilian developments had closed all but the richest workings in India. Up to 1895 the yield from South African diamond fields was thirteen tons, valued at £60,000,000. The diamondiferous soil of these parts changes at a depth of 100 or 150 feet from a soft, loamy, yellowish earth to a hard blue clay, the real matrix, which crumbles on exposure to the air. The mass as taken from the mine, after being thus disintegrated, is reduced to such small compass by rotary washing machines that the precious stones are readily discovered.

The Kimberley mine, first known as the Colesberg Koppij, though not so large as the De Beers, one mile distant, is the richest of them all. The claims staked out in January, 1871, had in 1874 reached a depth of 100 feet, when water and caving became troublesome. Open working on the De Beers mine reached a depth of 450 feet in 1885, and later in underground working a depth of 1,200 feet was attained. The blue earth is raised by engines, and carried to a hill for the exposure which causes disintegration. Open workings in

OPEN WORKINGS, KIMBERLEY DIAMOND MINES

the Bultfontein mine near by have reached a depth of 700 feet. The Dutoitspan mine, also close at hand, has produced the largest stone, 404 carats, or more than three ounces; the largest diamond from the De Beers mine was a yellow stone weighing 302 carats, while the most valuable one, called the Porter-Rhodes, a white octahedron weighing 150 carats and valued at £60,000, came from the Kimberley.

Gambling attended early diamond-digging in Africa as with early gold-digging in California. There were the usual games, roulette, rouge-et-noir, trente-et-quarante, and faro, conducted openly in houses of good repute, one saloon making £40,000 within a few months. With government prohibition at Kimberley, gamblers betook themselves across the Orange Free State line to Wessel's farm, near Dutoitspan, which place later became notorious for its illicit diamond traffic. Race-course lotteries were next in vogue; but public gaming at the diamond mines was neither heavy nor long protracted. The illicit traffic in diamonds continued, however, with increasing proportions until in 1882, when stringent laws were passed and a detective agency established, it was estimated that not more than half of the diamond yield had reached the owners of the mines. The precautions since adopted have rendered stealing almost impossible, the miners being stripped and closely examined at the end of each day's work.

KAFIR COMPOUND, DE BEERS DIAMOND MINES, KIMBERLEY

The town of Kimberley, with 30,000 people, to which may be added Beaconsfield with 10,000, has been built with little regard to regularity of streets; yet it contains some presentable edifices which have taken the place of those at first constructed of corrugated iron, notably the high court building of Griqualand West, and the public library. Never was there so much mining in progress throughout the world as at the present day, when aside from American and Australian outputs, a steady stream of gold is pouring into London from Africa, causing an excitement as deep if not as boisterous as any South Sea or Mississippi bubble. It is claimed for the principal mines that they contain true fissure veins, and if this be the case, no present estimate can be formed as to their prospective yield.

CHAPTER THE EIGHTEENTH

AUSTRALIA, THE HAWAIIAN ISLANDS

Where is the Austral Fatherland?
Behold it here, that mighty land!
Where Tasman's island sleeps at ease,
Far north toward the Timor seas;
From the great barrier's coral shoals,
To where the Indian ocean rolls;
From coral sea to ocean sand —
That is the Austral Fatherland.
    — *Australian Marseillaise.*

 He has even gone so far us to reproach me with my poverty — a charge truly acceptable to a philosopher, and one to which I readily plead guilty. For poverty has long been the handmaid of philosophy; frugal, temperate, contented with little, eager for praise, averse from the things sought by wealth, safe in her ways, simple in her requirements, in her counsels a promoter of what is right. No one has she ever puffed up with pride, no one has she corrupted by the enjoyment of power, no one has she maddened with tyrannical ambition; for no pampering of the appetite or of the passions does she sigh, nor can she indulge it. But it is your fosterings of wealth who are in the habit of perpetrating these disgraceful excesses, and others of a kindred nature. If you review all the greatest enormities that have been committed in the memory of mankind, you will not find a single poor man among the perpetrators; whilst, on the other hand, in the number of illustrious men hardly any of the rich are to be found; poverty has nurtured from his very cradle every individual in whom we find anything to admire and commend. Poverty, I say — she who in former ages was the foundress of all cities, the inventress of all arts, she who is guiltless of all offence, who is lavish of all glory, who has been honored with every praise among all nations. For this same poverty it was that, among the Greeks, showed herself just in Aristides, humane in Phocion, resolute in Epaminondas, wise in Socrates, and eloquent in Homer. I could, indeed, mass an argument with you about the very name itself, and I could show that none of us are poor who do not wish for superfluities, and who possess the things that are necessary, which, by nature, are but few indeed. For he has the most who desires the least; he who wants but little is most likely to have as much as he wants. — *Apuleius.*

 ABOUT the middle of the sixteenth century the captain of a French vessel voyaging in the southern seas landed on the western coast of Australia, not for purposes of trader or settlement, but merely to gratify his curiosity. The captain must have happened on an unfavorable spot; for his report was in substance as follows: Extending in all directions as far as the eye could reach were dense forests of gum-exuding trees in which were neither fruits nor herbs nor anything that would support existence. There were strange looking animals with short fore-legs and long sinuous hind-legs, carrying their young in pouches and sitting squat on the ground, from which, when startled, they rose with tremendous leaps, jumping twenty feet or more at a single bound. As to the natives, they were so nearly akin to the beasts in habits and appearance that it was doubtful whether they should be classed with the human or brute creation. While this was the first recorded discovery, there are allusions at least as early as the days of Alexander to a Terra Australis, or south land, at some future day to be revealed. In the writings of Strabo and Pliny there is also mention of this mysterious region, while Ptolemy believed it to be the southern bound of the Indian ocean, which he supposed to be an inland sea. Such were the popular notions of Australia until after the close of the middle ages, though travellers in China, and especially Marco Polo, brought back reports of a vast insular continent toward the southeast.

The accidental discovery of Torres, who early in the seventeenth century sailed through the strait which bears his name, was followed by Dutch and English explorations, prominent among which were those of Tasman, Dampier, and Cook. On the 20th of January, 1777, the last named of these navigators planted the British flag on the shore of Botany bay, so called by one of the savans of the expedition on account of the number and novelty of the botanical specimens in the neighborhood; the extensive coast line explored by Cook, together with the country back of it, receiving the name of New South Wales. Returning homeward, the latter spoke in glowing terms of the sunny skies, the pure, elastic atmosphere, and the wondrous plant-life of the Austral land, his statements leading to further expeditions and to further discoveries.

After the loss of her American colonies, Great Britain was in need of a place to which to transport the criminals formerly shipped to the western plantations and settlements. Botany bay was the spot selected, mainly through the representations of Cook; and thence went, toward the close of 1787, a fleet of eleven sail, with more than a thousand persons on board, the most of them being convicts. Arthur Phillip, the first governor of New South Wales, was in charge of the expedition. But the site was found to be unsuitable; the anchorage was unsafe; fresh water was scarce, and the narrow strip of open land that skirted the shore was surrounded with swamp and forest. Proceeding a few miles northward in search of a more favorable spot, Phillip entered Port Jackson, named after the sailor who first descried it, and then supposed to be a small, unsheltered inlet. But after passing between its lofty heads, he found himself in one of the most spacious and beautiful harbors in the world, its waters widening into a broad, unruffled expanse, studded with wooded islets and indented with rock-encircled coves. To the inmost basin of this harbor the flotilla was transferred; tents were erected on the shore adjacent; and thus was founded, on the 26th of January, 1778, the city of Sydney, the oldest of Australian settlements and at present the second in population and wealth.

SYDNEY

Other colonies were presently established — those later known as Victoria and South and West Australia — and other settlements founded, as Melbourne on Hobson bay and Adelaide near the gulf of St. Vincent, though for more than a quarter of a century the inhabited portion was limited to the plain adjacent to Sydney, some fifty miles in width, between the Blue mountains and the shore of the south Pacific. Of the earlier explorers, many lost their lives in this almost impassable range, covered with trackless forests to a height of more than 3,000 feet, and intersected with precipitous ravines. Nevertheless explorations were continued, and are still continued, the results of which, though yet far from complete, may thus be briefly stated.

MELBOURNE

The longest line that can be drawn in Australia is from east to west and 2,600 miles in length, the extreme width from north to south being nearly 2,000 miles, and the area some 2,000,000,000 acres, or about the same as that of the United States excluding the territory of Alaska. In its 9,000 miles of shore line there are few good harbors, except on the northern side, where the gulf of Carpentaria forms an opening 400 miles long, and as much in width, though less protected than other and smaller inlets. It is probable that in an age not far remote, as geological ages are computed, the interior was the bed of an inland sea, the mountains forming the cliffs and plateaus of many island groups, such as those of the Pacific archipelagoes. In support of this theory are the thinness of the soil and the erratic course of the rivers, several of which, after running far inward from the coast ranges, lose themselves in swamps or shallow lakes, their channels in the dry season become mere chains of ponds. At least two-thirds of the surface is little better than desert. In the eastern section are by far the most valuable lands, and in general terms it may be stated that there are no large areas that can be utilized, even for the grazing of sheep, more than a few hundred miles from the coast.

In a continent extending over nearly 40 degrees of longitude and 30 of latitude there might be expected a great diversity of climate; but such is not the case, except as to rainfall, which varies from 40 inches or more on portions of the coast to an occasional sprinkling in the interior deserts. In Australia, as the saying goes, it is always a flood or a drought, the latter sometimes lasting for two or three years in succession, and attended with enormous destruction of crops and live-stock; for there is no irrigation worthy of the name, nor is irrigation possible in a land where the rivers are few and small, and where snow is seen only on the highest mountain peaks. The mean annual temperature of Sydney is 66°, of Melbourne about 58°; but in both these cities the thermometer occasionally rises above 100° in the shade, and far above that point in the interior, hot winds laden with dust and thence called "brickfielders" blowing for two or three days at a time. These are often followed by violent electric disturbances accompanied with torrents of rain, one of the severest ever known occurring in January 1886, when towns were swept out of existence in a night, and their neighborhood for many miles around was ablaze with globes and streams of light moving in waves like an aurora, but with awful intensity. In other respects the country is remarkable; Christmas is the Australian midsummer; in winter the trees shed their bark instead of their foliage, the leaves expanding vertically so as to afford but little shade, while there are fruits that grow with the stone outside, and animals that combine the properties of the bird and beast creation.

Of the 10,000 species of plants included in the Australian flora there are none that will support life, except wild fruits and edible roots, even these being few. The forests are of vast extent, and in places the forest scenery is strikingly magnificent, especially in the Blue mountains, where is a landscape view with waterfalls approaching in grandeur the famed Yosemite of the Californian sierra. In addition to the omnipresent gum-tree, there are many varieties of merchantable timber, as the Moreton bay pine, the iron-bark, the oak, red cedar, rosewood, sandal-wood, and satin-wood. Of animals the kangaroo, opossum, dingo, and native bear are the most common, the last being undersized and resembling a sloth in its habits. Wild ducks and other aquatic fowl are plentiful, the black swan being here so little of a rarity as to belie the Latin proverb. The emu, now almost extinct, resembles somewhat the African ostrich; there are countless swarms of noisy parrots and cockatoos, some of the former exceedingly beautiful; but more beautiful than any is the lyrebird, belonging to the same order as the bird of paradise, and so-called from its tail feathers, which spread in the form of a lyre. The coast and inland waters of Australia, and especially those of New South Wales, are abundantly stocked with fish. With metals and minerals, both precious and useful, the country is well supplied, and these are as yet but in the infancy of their development.

From about 1,000 in 1787 the population of Australia had increased to 175,000 in 1851, at which date there returned to its shores, among other disappointed gold-seekers from California, one Edward Hargraves by name. Happening on the neighborhood of Summerhill creek, in the Macquarie plains, a few leagues north of Bathurst, he observed there geological formations closely resembling those which he had seen in California placers, and selecting the most promising spot, straightway began to dig. The stroke of his pick has become historic, and has also been exceedingly profitable; for it has resulted thus far in the addition of $1,750,000,000 to the world's stock of the precious metals. A few months later other fields were discovered, as those of Ballarat, Bendigo, and Anderson creek, all within a hundred miles of Melbourne. There were disclosed in New South Wales, the deposits known to exist many years before, but kept secret for fear of their effect on a penal colony. The result of these discoveries was similar to that which was witnessed in California two or three years before, settlers from far and near deserting their farms and shops by thousands to search for the treasure which all men covet. The news was quickly spread throughout the world, and from a hundred ports ships laden with passengers, stores, and implements were headed for Hobson bay, where presently were repeated the scenes of 1849 in the city and harbor of the Golden Gate.

Victoria has produced about 80 per cent of the entire yield of Australian gold, New South Wales contributing less than 13 per cent, though in the latter colony the formations in which gold is usually found cover an area of 70,000 square miles. But her capitalists are loath to venture their money, and her miners and metallurgists have much to learn. Says the under secretary of the mining department in a recent report, "When account is taken of the number of mines standing idle because we do not know how to treat the ore, and the value of the metals that are wasted in the treatment of ores through ignorance of the methods by which such metals could be saved, some idea may be formed of the amount which our output might under favorable circumstances be reasonably expected to reach."

Among historic nuggets the first one was found by a sheepherder in New South Wales in 1851. It was sold for £1,000, or about one-fifth of its value, for it weighed more than 100 pounds; but this was perhaps all the better for the shepherd, who within a few weeks returned to his task after expending the entire sum in carousing, as is squandered nearly all the money earned or otherwise obtained by Australian shepherds. More sensible were the two laborers who a score of years later, while resting beneath a tree in one of the Victoria gold fields, chanced on a £10,000 nugget lying loose, and straightway lodged it in a bank. Sarah Sands was the name given to one of the largest lumps unearthed at Ballarat, weighing 150 pounds and worth more than £6,000, though a 184 pound nugget is said to have come from that camp, while rumor hath it that in New South Wales was found in 1872 a lump of solid gold weighing 640 pounds. But here we will stop; for nugget stories, like fish stories must be taken with certain grains of allowance.

While the alluvial gold fields of Australia have for the most part been abandoned, quartz-mining maintains a diminished but very considerable yield. Victoria still promises to add largely year by year to the £270,000,000 already produced in that colony, ores assaying less than a quarter of an ounce to the ton being worked at a profit under careful treatment and honest management. In New South Wales it is the belief of mining experts that the surface of the country has been merely scratched, and certain it is that new discoveries are constantly being made in localities supposed to have been thoroughly exploited. Many companies are working in a quiet way and paying handsome dividends, about which nothing is said. Not long ago 115 pounds' weight of gold was extracted from 10 tons of rock, a slab of vein stuff that weighed about a quarter of a ton yielding £2,000. In another mine, from 436 tons of ore were produced 27,000 ounces, valued at £93,000; but these are of course exceptional instances. Queensland had in 1895 one of the largest gold mines in the world, producing to that date about 60,000,000 ounces and paying as much as £1,000,000 a year in dividends. Mount Morgan, it is called, the location being south of the town of Rockhampton. Of ore yielding three to twelve ounces there were said to be many millions of tons in sight, though the gold was so finely distributed as to be invisible to the naked eye. In the peninsula of Cape York, not far from the extreme north-eastern point of Queensland and of Australia, there are believed to be deposits of the precious metals still awaiting the advent of the prospector and the capitalist, far richer than any yet developed.

New South Wales takes the lead in production of silver and silver-lead ores, exporting to the value of some £3,000,000 a year, apart from those which are worked at home. Between 1886 and 1892 there were disbursed by the Broken Hill mines, accidentally discovered by the boundary rider of a sheep farm, nearly £4,000,000 in dividends, or at the rate of £260 to each £9 share of stock, the total yield up to the latter date being 36,500,000 ounces of silver and 150,000 tons of lead. If such results had been achieved in the mines which have brought poverty on thousands of Californians, the world would never have heard the last of it; yet while the Comstock lode is world famous, there are comparatively few who have heard even that silver mines exist in the Australias.

The total production of copper, up to 1895, mainly from the Burra Burra and Moonta mines in South Australia, was valued at £28,000,000, the colony exporting in former years a vast amount of high-grade ores, while Queensland was also a large producer; but with a fall in copper from £170 to less than £50 a ton, and also through the manipulation of speculative syndicates, the yield has greatly diminished. Tin worth £600,000 is produced in a twelve-month, and of this a considerable proportion is shipped in ingots to the United States. In New South Wales alone there are more than 100 coal mines, whose product has already realized more than £30,000,000, the annual output varying from 3,000,000 to 4,000,000 tons a year. The best mines are in the neighborhood of Newcastle, a seaport north of Sydney, the average price of coal at the mouth of the pit not exceeding the equivalent of $2.25 a ton, though the earnings of the miner are much larger than in the United States.

Among the free settlers who landed in Sydney in 1803 was Captain John Macarthur, to whom, as is related, King George III presented ten fine merino sheep. Macarthur had travelled much, in Saxony among other lands, and he observed that Australian grasses resembled closely those of that famous wool-growing country. Purchasing, therefore, a few choice rams and ewes imported from Cape colony, he secured a tract of land and applied himself to the business of rearing fine-wool sheep. Here was the inception of the greatest of Australian industries, Macarthur's score or two of sheep proving to be many a golden fleece; for there are now at least 120,000,000 sheep in Australia, representing, with the stations or farms on which they are pastured, a value of £450,000,000. Nearly half this number are in New South Wales, and here as elsewhere are many squatters, as they are termed, with incomes of from £20,000 to £100,000 a year, while of a pastoral king who is the owner of 30 stations in various counties and colonies, it is said that his annual revenue seldom falls short of £200,000. Among the larger class of squatters a man who makes less than £10,000 a year considers himself in danger of the almshouse, 50,000 acres being considered as quite a small station, while there are not a few of 1,000,000 acres or more, leased from the government at an average yearly rate of less than a halfpenny an acre. As a sheep can be fed on five or six acres and will yield at each clip several shillings' worth of wool, it will be seen that there is room for profit in the business. But losses are frequent and severe; in seasons of protracted drought a band of 2,000 or 3,000 sheep can be had for the asking, without money or price, by anyone who will drive them away; for there is neither food nor water to keep them alive. Moreover, the rich Australian squatter is a man of extravagant habits and much given to hospitality, expending yearly many thousands of pounds on his guests, his family, and himself. Yet he may have begun his career with only a few hundred pounds of capital, while some have begun with nothing, taking up land and purchasing a flock of sheep on credit.

Cattle farming, though on a large scale and yielding fair returns, is a less frequent and profitable industry. There are about 12,000,000 horned cattle in Australia, or more than three per capita of the population, a larger proportion than in any other of the old or new world continents. While large quantities of frozen and tinned meats are shipped to Great Britain, yet larger quantities go to waste, stock being killed by millions in seasons of drought, and sold for whatever their hides, pelts, wool, and tallow are worth. A single firm in New South Wales has facilities for handling 1,500,000 carcasses a year, and there are many smaller establishments; for the growth of this industry is limited only by the demand. After providing for local requirements, at least 250,000 cattle and 5,000,000 sheep could be exported yearly in the form of meats from the natural increase in flocks and herds.

The total value of all agricultural products varies from £25,000,000 to £30,000,000 a year, or an average of some £3 per acre under crop, wheat ranking first with a production worth £6,000,000; maize about £1,500,000, and barley, oats and other cereals £2,500,000; while of hay the yield is worth £5,000,000 and of vegetables £3,500,000. Of wheat 10 bushels an acre is considered a fair crop; of maize 25, and of oats 20 bushels. There are few large grain farmers in Australia, most of the agricultural holdings being less than 150 acres, while in New South Wales, the oldest of the colonies, not one per cent of its area is under cultivation. Most of the land is leased at a nominal rent to men engaged in the raising of live-stock; but the leases are short, and all pastoral districts are subject to preemption by bona fide settlers at moderate rates and on payments long deferred. Of fruits there is an enormous crop, the product of orchards and vineyards being estimated at £4,000,000 a year, though for want of markets, much of it is fed to hogs and more is left to rot on the ground. Manufactures, though rapidly increasing, are not as yet of large amount, and almost entirely for home consumption. But of the resources, industries, and commerce of the various colonies further mention will be made elsewhere in MISCELLANY of this chapter. Meanwhile let us turn to the cities and towns of the southern continent, some of them already of metropolitan rank.

From a mere convict settlement, founded as I have said in 1788, Sydney has developed into a city of 425,000 inhabitants, and with a large volume of commerce, industries, and wealth, imports and exports exceeding £50,000,000 a year, while the assessed value of property is at the rate of £500 per capita, and money is at times so plentiful in the banks that they refuse to pay interest on new deposits. "The city of a hundred bays" it has been called; nor is the title undeserved; for in its harbor, extending fifteen miles in one direction and nine in another, are innumerable sheltered coves. On one of these, named Sydney cove, near the head of which is the business centre, was built the Circular quay, the largest of many wharves, and with accommodation for scores of sea-going ships. While there are many narrow and tortuous streets, flanked with the old-fashioned buildings in which the earlier colonists were content to dwell, others, laid out on regular lines, are bordered with handsome and costly structures, granite and polished marble being largely used among other ornamental details, betokening the wealth and taste of the community. There are many beautiful suburbs, and parks and recreation grounds are numerous, chief among them being the Domain, with its sightly botanic gardens and aviary, where nature and art combine in forming one of the most attractive public resorts in the world.

PRINCE ALBERT, SYDNEY

In what is known as the inner Domain, overlooking the harbor and in the midst of ornamental gardens and parklike scenery, is Government house, designed in part by the architect of Buckingham palace. In this residence of the viceroy, resembling externally a castle rather than a viceregal mansion, the state apartments are tastefully decorated, and the private rooms furnished with due regard to comfort and elegance. Most of the modern public buildings are in imitation of the classic style, though somewhat florid, especially the town hall, in which is the largest assembly room in Australia, capable of seating 5,000 persons. The post-office is a stately edifice, 353 feet in length, 110 feet at its widest point, and surmounted by a tower whose summit is 245 feet above the pavement. Its cost was about £300,000, and in design it is largely individual, as are not a few of its neighbors; for in Australia sameness and deformity of plan are not considered, as in the United States, essential to government architecture. The Lands office, on which £200,000 was expended, is a freestone structure of the composite order, 200 by 280 feet, fronting on four thoroughfares, surrounded by a handsome peristyle and capped with a large octagonal dome. For the offices of the colonial secretary and the secretary of public works was erected at an outlay of £130,000 a building which for symmetry of proportion and elegance of detail may be termed the architectural gem of the metropolis. The museum, with its mineral and other collections, was designed as a miniature reproduction of the British museum; the Catholic cathedral is the finest of church edifices, and the university is a Gothic composition with a spacious and lofty hall whose roof presents one of the finest specimens of the carver's art.

There are many tasteful villas in the outskirts of Sydney, and in the city itself are imposing business blocks, with shops and hotels that would be no discredit to a European metropolis, though the days are not long gone by when there was not a single hostelry ranking above the second class, not a single restaurant of any kind, nor a single mile of cable-road. Of late the people have awakened in a measure from the lethargy of earlier days. Population has more than doubled within the last quarter of a century, and wealth has increased three or four fold, the capitalized value of real property, including the immediate suburbs, exceeding £120,000,000 and the rental £6,500,000. Yet, as compared with the Americans, and even with neighboring communities, they are an easy-going and somnolent folk, lacking in enterprise and ambition. Between three and four o'clock business is over for the day, whereupon everyone devotes himself to his favorite recreation; some to the cricket field in Hyde park, others to yachting or boating, and yet others to driving or horseback riding. Public holidays are numerous and universally celebrated, while never a week-day passes in the summer season but steamers laden with holiday makers speed across the harbor to some favorite picnic ground. Living is cheaper than in the United States, so that a bachelor can get along comfortably on £100 a year, and on £150 he may marry if so inclined, his wife expending on herself not more than £15 or £20 a year, and with that sum dressing in neater and more elegant attire than the daughter of a millionaire in some countries. Sydney is one of the most quiet and orderly of towns; for while a large proportion of the inhabitants are the offspring or descendants of convicts, these are among the wealthiest, best educated, and best behaved of citizens, their estates coming largely by inheritance from men who, after serving their sentence, received grants of land, which after the gold discovery commanded fabulous prices.

Brisbane, the capital of Queensland, is the daughter of New South Wales, both city and district, the latter five times the size of the United Kingdom, belonging politically to the mother colony until 1859. From 25,000 inhabitants at that date, the population of

Queensland has increased to more than 500,000, about one-fourth of whom are residents of Brisbane and its suburbs on the river of that name, not far from its outlet into Moreton bay. While there are no very imposing edifices, there are many buildings of generous proportions and sightly aspect; nor is there anything wanting that is essential to social or business life. The clubs and churches, the educational, philanthropic, and charitable institutions are worthy of a larger and older community; there are a score at least of daily or weekly journals; there is a large and rapidly increasing commerce, and there is regular steam communication with other Australian ports, especially with Sydney, some 500 miles to the south.

In 1835 a party of adventurers crossing Bass strait from Tasmania, or Van Diemen's land as then it was called, built on the opposite shore, near the banks of a small stream named the Yarra Yarra a cluster of wooden huts, supporting themselves by fishing and raising such meagre crops as the neighboring soil would produce. Thus was founded the city of Melbourne, the metropolis of the Australias, and among the largest and most thriving commercial seaports in the world, from whose harbor of Port Phillip — resembling rather an inland sea, for in its centre no land is visible — gold has been shipped to the value of hundreds of millions of pounds. Melbourne with its suburbs, where are now the homes of some 550,000 people, was described by Anthony Trollope, as "One of the most successful cities on the face of the earth;" and well it deserves that title; for beneath its clear, bright sky is everywhere the appearance of prosperity and comfort, — spacious and well kept thoroughfares, parks, and pleasure grounds lined or surrounded with elegant and costly residences, business blocks, banks, and public buildings, in which is represented no small portion of the £650,000,000 of capital accumulated in the Australasian colonies.

The city proper is built on the slopes and summits of two parallel hills, together with the valley between them, where is the business quarter, with its principal thoroughfares 90 feet wide and a furlong apart, between which are narrower streets. Around the city and within a radius of five or six miles from the general post-office is a circle of populous suburbs, many of them forming independent municipalities, and not a few with streets and shops almost as busy as those of the business centre. Parks, squares, and gardens are numerous, and some of them are lavishly decorated, Fitzroy gardens, for instance, in the very heart of the metropolis, containing avenues of oak and elm separated by Fern-tree gully, and with summer-houses, fountains, ponds, miniature Greek temples, and replicas of famous statuary. There is also vacant land for sale to those who are willing to pay £40,000 or £50,000 for half-acre allotments, which sold in 1837 for £35 apiece. Thus it is that the capital of Victoria, with only one-tenth the population of the capital of Great Britain, occupies an area nearly half as large.

No city of its size, and few cities anywhere in the world, contain so many handsome public buildings as Melbourne; San Francisco, for example, with similar origin and much greater natural advantages, being altogether unworthy of comparison in this and other respects. The oldest and one of the finest is the post-office, though as yet incomplete, for its plan provides for an addition to be used as the headquarters of the telegraph system under government control. In the town-hall is a chamber with seating capacity for 3,000 persons, and with a colossal organ on which afternoon performances are given. For the law-courts an imposing structure has recently been erected, its elaborate facades, 300 feet in length, surmounted by a lofty cupola resembling that of the capitol at Washington. The new houses of parliament with their freestone fronts, their Doric colonnade, and rich interior decorations, form a plain but dignified composition. The treasury and mint are well proportioned edifices, the latter adding millions of sovereigns a year to the gold circulation of the colony. In a structure remarkable chiefly for hugeness of dimensions are the principal government offices. The public library is a creditable specimen of colonial architecture. On the lower story are sculpture and picture galleries containing reproductions and original works of art, with many thousands of engravings, photographs, and illustrations of the industrial arts. On the upper floor are 150,000 volumes arranged in recesses provided for every branch of literature, and where the visitor may roam at will so long as he keeps silence and replaces books where he found them. The university is housed in a picturesque group of no great size, the finest being Wilson hall, which divides with the Scotch kirk the architectural honors of Melbourne. The anglican and catholic cathedrals are among the best of many church buildings; and there are colleges, hospitals, theatres, hotels, and other edifices in keeping with a city of metropolitan rank.

PARLIAMENT HOUSE, MELBOURNE

There are other towns on this inland sea named Port Phillip, chief among which is Geelong, co-existent with Melbourne as a settlement, and pleasantly situated on the western arm of the bay. Its streets are regular and spacious, and there are many stately buildings, with parks, botanical gardens, and other adjuncts such as befit a town that was once the rival of Melbourne. Less than sixty miles northwest of Geelong and connected with it by rail is Ballarat, "the golden city" it has been termed and as Anthony Trollope remarked more than a score of years ago, "in point of architectural excellence and civilized comfort the metropolis of the Australian gold-fields." Instead of searching for low-grade ore, as now they do at a depth of more than 2,000 feet, the miners of olden days were accustomed to take out several thousand pounds from claims a few feet square, a single tubful of earth yielding as much £3,225. Not far away is Bendigo, the centre of an auriferous district extending over 150 square miles, and containing immense deposits of gold-bearing quartz.

Adelaide, the capital and only important city of south Australia, is built on the banks of the Torrens, a few miles from its outlet into the gulf of St. Vincent. Though small, it is one of the most sightly of cities, with a background of wooded mountains 2,500 feet in height, while almost in its centre the river, spanned by several bridges, divides the residence and business sections, the former containing the neatest of villas interspersed with churches and colleges. Many of the public edifices were erected by Melbourne architects, and are in excellent taste, especially the town-hall, court-house, post-office, and museum, where are large collections of minerals and specimens in natural history. Worthy of mention also are the new houses of parliament and the university building, the latter a Gothic structure with spacious hall and lecture rooms; nor should we forget the park lands which encircle the town, nearly 2,000 acres in extent, and the botanical gardens in the eastern suburb, the pride of the south Australian. There is a clean, fresh look about Adelaide, with its vine-clad residences, its perfect drainage system, and its abundance of pure water, making it probably the healthiest city on the continent.

Perth, like Sydney, was founded as a convict settlement, though transportation to western Australia ceased in 1868, and to New South Wales thirty years before, the people of Victoria threatening to land a cargo of their own criminals on British shores for each one that should he sent from Britain to the former colony. Nearly one-half of the 60,000 inhabitants of western Australia reside in Perth or Freemantle, the former, built partly with convict labor, being the capital city. It has many commodious buildings, both public and private, including protestant and catholic cathedrals, a town-hall, library, state grammar school, government offices, and the official residence of the governor.

Tasmania, originally a penal colony founded in 1803 as a branch of the New South Wales establishment, is now the home of thousands of contented and prosperous farmers, whose thrifty homesteads, orchards, and fields of grain, in valleys and plateaus surrounded with verdure-clad hills, recall the beauties of English landscape scenery. Well does it deserve its title of "the garden of Australia;" for here can be raised all fruits and plants that thrive on British soil, together with the vine, the fig, and other semi-tropical products. Wheat averages 17 bushels and oats nearly 30 bushels to the acre, while of potatoes four or five tons are an average yield, and on the northwest coast as much may be harvested from a single rood of land. In 1895 the island contained about 175,000 horned cattle and 1,600,000 sheep, while the country abounds with game and the coast and inland waters with fish. Of its mineral resources I have already spoken, and these, in common with others, need only capital and enterprise for their profitable development.

In beauty of site there are few more favored cities than Hobart Town, the capital, built on more hills than Rome itself, and overlooking the stately stream of the Derwent a few miles above its outlet. There are many churches, chief among which are the catholic and protestant cathedrals; there are charitable institutions supported by the state, and in the business quarter are several banks; for there are many rich men in Hobart Town, notwithstanding its sleepy and self-contented aspect. The public buildings are adjacent to each other, and in the suburbs is Government house, a castellated mansion whose grounds adjoin the botanic gardens. Launceston, on the northern and opposite side of the colony, is connected by rail with the capital and by steamer with Melbourne, which can be reached in few hours' trip. It has also its public buildings, its town-hall, hospitals, library, theatre, and the rest, one of the oldest structures being the episcopal church erected in 1824. In the railroad journey across the island, though made to better advantage by coach, as in earlier days, is some of the finest scenery that human eye can rest upon.

New Zealand is also noted for its magnificent landscape views, grand rather than beautiful; for the foliage is of sombre hue, forest-clad mountains covering a large proportion of the North island, while in the South island the Southern Alps and cither ranges occupy four-fifths of its area. On their eastern side are extensive and fertile plains; on their western slope are inexhaustible stores of mineral wealth, and on the southwestern coast fiords, long, narrow, and deep, encircled with snow clad peaks, give to this region all the sublimity of Norwegian or Alaskan scenery. There is an abundant rainfall; rivers and lakes are numerous and in all portions of the country are running streams of the purest water. The climate is equable in the main and with no great extremes of heat or cold, though of course with the usual variations caused by latitude, elevation, and exposure, the mean annual temperature of the entire colony being 63° in summer and 48° in winter. It is a healthy land, one of the healthiest in the world, the death rate not exceeding 11 per 1,000, or very much less than in Great Britain or Australia.

While the resources and industries of New Zealand and Australia have much in common, there is little common as to their fauna and flora. In the former country not only are marsupials unknown, but there are no indigenous animals of any kind except the native dog and rat. There are about 140 species of birds peculiar to New Zealand, including the moa, a huge wingless creature of the genus dinornis, believed to have been as much as twelve feet high, but now extinct. The eucalyptus, which covers so large a portion of the Australian continent, is unknown in New Zealand; but in its place is the Kauri pine, together with 120 species of indigenous evergreens, among which are many of economic value. Wide tracts are covered with grasses suitable for the pasturage of cattle and sheep, the former being at least 1,000,000 and the latter 25,000,000 in number. Including the very large area sown with imported grasses, there are 11,000,000 acres under crop, and there is more than that quantity of good agricultural land still at the disposal of whosoever will purchase it from the crown. Of wheat an average yield is 23 bushels, and of oats and barley from 28 to 30 bushels an acre. Minerals are widely distributed, the production of gold being at the rate of nearly £1,000,000 a year, of coal £400,000, and there are valuable deposits of copper, iron, lead, zinc, and antimony, for the most part still untouched.

Auckland is the largest town, containing about one-fifth of the 325,000 inhabitants of the North island. It is a thriving little seaport and is surrounded with thriving villages, with which it is connected by rail. Among its principal buildings are the governor's mansion and the cathedral, a wharf nearly half a mile in length affording excellent accommodation for shipping. Christ church, on South island, which together with Stewart island to the south contains nearly 400,000 people, is a railroad centre in the midst of the great Canterbury plain. It is also a prosperous agricultural town with many handsome buildings, and connected with it by rail is its port of Lyttleton.

AUCKLAND

Dunedin, on Otago harbor, has a considerable shipping and local trade, its customs revenue amounting to some £500,000 a year. It is beautifully situated amid an amphitheatre of hills, and has wide and well paved streets, built at great expense through swamps and ridges. Among its many fine edifices are the presbyterian churches, the university of Otago, and the museum, where is an exhaustive collection of New Zealand flora and fauna. There are many other towns in this prosperous colony, where poverty is rare and destitution unknown; but as one is like unto another, they need not here be mentioned in detail.

In the light of recent events the Hawaiian islands have become of more than usual interest, especially to Americans, among whom their history, physical features, resources, and products are too well known to require extended description. As to their annals, they differ not from those of many other lands which have fallen under foreign domination under the name of a protectorate or such euphemistic phrase as may cloak the iniquity of taking by force what belongs to another. First came the missionaries to convert some 140,000 natives, now reduced to less than one-fourth of that number through the importation of European vices. These they termed savages, though a light-hearted and good-natured folk, and leading a far more natural life than the missionaries themselves; naked but not ashamed, and subsisting almost without labor on the spontaneous fruits of the earth. In the wake of the missionaries followed traders and capitalists, picking up all that could be had for little or nothing in the way of lands and commodities. Finally came revolution, with proposed annexation to some foreign power.

The islands are mainly of volcanic origin, and most of them are extremely mountainous; but there are large areas of fertile land especially suitable for the production of sugar. Coffee, fruits, and wool are also among exports averaging perhaps $12,000,000 a year, against imports of half that amount, the trade being almost entirely with the United States and to a small extent with Australia, a regular and subsidized line of steamers connecting the islands with both these countries and also with New Zealand. There is a moderate volume of internal commerce, and there are about 60 miles of railroad and 300 of telegraph line, the laying of a cable between the various islands and thence extended to the American and Australian continents being one of the projects under contemplation in 1897. Government is expensive for so small a community, less than 100,000 in all; and here was the principal cause of the revolution; for a large proportion of the revenue, sometimes exceeding $2,000,000 a year, was appropriated for the expenses of the royal family, whose manner of living was somewhat extravagant.

KING KALAKAUA

Hawaii is the largest of the group, its area of 4,200 square miles covering two-thirds of their entire surface. It is almost entirely occupied with the slopes of volcanic mountains with gentle ascent and forest-clad to a height of 6,000 feet. Mauna Loa and Kilauea are its active volcanoes, the latter being the largest in the world, its crater, nearly ten miles in circumference and with vertical walls 1,000 feet in height filled with a lake of molten lava. An eruption of Mauna Loa in 1868 was attended with earthquakes and a tidal wave 40 feet in height, causing much loss of life and property, while in the same year another wave, crossing the Pacific from the coast of South America, not only struck the islands but made itself felt as far as the coasts of Australia and New Zealand. Hilo, the largest settlement, on an open roadstead of that name protected by a coral reef, is little better than a village, around which are many thriving plantations.

NATIVE HOUSE, HAWAIIAN ISLANDS

Honolulu, on the island of Oahu, is remarkable rather for the beauty of its site than for its buildings, many of which are one-story frame houses, and not a few are merely huts of grass. Nevertheless, it has its royal palace, formerly the residence of the king; its churches, business structures, and benevolent associations, the foreign and especially the American element being the dominant power in the land. Oahu is a beautiful island, its peaks, cliffs, and cascades, its valleys and lower mountain slopes clad with tropical vegetation presenting all the elements of the picturesque. Kauai is also famous for its scenery, and for its fertile soil of decomposed lava. In Maui is the extinct volcano of Haleakala, that is to say "the home of the sun," more than 10,000 feet in height, with a crater 2,700 feet from top to rim, and a surface area of nearly 16 square miles. In Molokai, with its leper settlement; in Lanai, Niihau, and other islands, there is nothing that need further detain us.

ROYAL PALACE, HONOLULU

MISCELLANY. — Of some of the innumerable islands and island groups between the Asiatic, Australian, and American continents mention has been made in the chapter on Central and Southeastern Asia. In conclusion a few words may be added as to the Fiji islands, more than 200 in number, the largest, named Viti Leru, having an area about equal to that of Jamaica. The native population exceeds 100,000, though rapidly decreasing, as appears to be the fate of Polynesian races when brought into contact with Europeans, of whom there are several thousands, with 12,000 or 15,000 laborers, largely imported for the sugar plantations under contracts which virtually make slaves of them. There are perhaps £5,000,000 of foreign capital invested, mainly in sugar industries, the trade of about £1,000,000 a year being almost exclusively with Australasia.

SUGAR-CANE PLANTATION, FIJI

Australasia, it is claimed, is the richest country in the world; private wealth, to say nothing of unsold government lands and public works, being valued in 1895 at £1,350,000,000, or more than £350 per capita of the population. For the same year the following figures as to the productions of the principal colonies may be accepted as approximately correct. New South Wales, agriculture, £4,500,000; stock-raising, £15,000,000; dairy farming, £3,000,000; mining, £5,500,000; forests and fisheries, £1,500,000. Victoria, agriculture, £8,500,000; stock-raising, £7,000,000; dairy farming, £4,000,000; mining, £3,000,000; forests and fisheries, £600,000. Queensland, agriculture, £2,500,000; stock-raising, £6,500,000; dairy farming, £1,100,000; mining, £2,800,000; forests and fisheries, £750,000. South Australia, agriculture, £3,750,000; stock-raising, £2,400,000; dairy farming, £850,000; mining £450,000; forests and fisheries, £350,000. New Zealand, agriculture, £5,500,000; stock-raising, £8,000,000; dairy farming, £2,250,000; mining, £1,750,000; forests and fisheries, £7,000,000. The figures for Western

Australia and Tasmania are very much smaller, and those for north Australia and Alexandraland comparatively insignificant.

For the year ending June 30, 1895, shipments of Australian and New Zealand wool amounted to 1,952,000 bales, against 1,890,000 in the preceding year, 70 per cent of the total being marketed in London, and 35,000 bales in the United States, where there is a moderate demand for the finer grades for admixture with those of coarser fibre.

The Australasian colonies are indebted to English capitalists probably to the amount of £400,000,000; but of this a large proportion is invested in railways and other public works under government control, already returning fair interest on the cost of construction and management, notwithstanding the sparse population.

At the entrance of the mining pavilion of New South Wales at the Columbian Exposition was a pillar of frosted silver from the Broken Hills mining company, its shaft festooned with garlands and supporting a figure of Atlas bearing his customary burden. In inscriptions on one of the walls was stated the mineral yield of the colony, including, up to the close of 1892, gold to the value of $187,000,000; silver and lead, $54,000,000; tin, $46,000,000; copper, $29,000,000; and coal $124,000,000, other products of the mine swelling the total to $500,000,000.

In Australia there have been several intercolonial expositions, and one or two which by a stretch of courtesy may he termed international. The last one was in Melbourne in 1888, in celebration of the founding of the first British settlement on Australian shores. The palace erected for the purpose is still preserved.

The university of Sydney has a government endowment of £12,000 a year and though a comparatively new institution, has already been enriched with donations and bequests exceeding £350,000. The president's salary, in addition to a handsome residence, is about £1,500, which was formerly also the annual stipend of a supreme court judge, though increased within recent years, the chief justice receiving £3,000, the attorney-general and colonial secretary each £2,000, and the governor £7,000.

In 1884 a company was formed to develop the diamond mines of New South Wales, and especially those at Bingera, with the result that 75,000 stones were found within three years, the largest weighing about six carats. The deposits are extensive, but have never been systematically worked, though Australian diamonds are of excellent quality, said to be superior to those of South Africa and Brazil.

On Thursday island, some 2,000 miles from Brisbane, some of the largest pearl beds in the world are worked by a joint-stock company on scientific principles and on an enormous scale. Some of the pearls are of extraordinary size and of beautiful lustre, occasional specimens selling for as much as £1,000 apiece, with many worth £100 and upward. On the pearl-fishing grounds of western Australia was found, in 1874, a group of nine pearls in the form of a Latin cross, and all of good size and color. It is said to have been recently sold for £10,400.

Tasmania, though not ranking high as a mining country, has produced, within the last quarter of a century, £2,500,000 in gold, a single company disbursing £500,000 in dividends, while at Rocky river nuggets have been found the largest of which weighed 240 and 143 ounces respectively. There are silver deposits giving promise of excellent returns; of tin the yield up to 1896 was valued at £8,000,000, and near tide-water on the eastern coast are 40,000 acres of coal lands.

Between 1886 and 1889 land speculation was rampant in Melbourne and elsewhere, caused largely by the influx of English capital borrowed for the construction of public works, among them the underground cable roads of the Tramway trust, whose members were appointed by the city and suburban councils. Then came the reaction, the effects of which were felt for several years, thousands who deemed themselves wealthy being driven to insolvency, and forfeiting, besides, their business reputation. The climax came in April 1893, when five of the principal banks suspended, with total liabilities exceeding £40,000,000, a terrible blow to the commerce and industries of all the colonies. In seasons of panic Australian banks will not stand by each other as do those of the United States.

RESOURCES

Learn more about Hubert Howe Bancroft

In addition to The Book of Wealth, Hubert Howe Bancroft wrote and published dozens of books on the history and settlement of the American West, the 1893 World's Fair and more.

To learn more about Bancroft and his business enterprises, the creation of the Bancroft Library at the University of California, Berkeley, and Bancroft's many other publications, visit:

www.BancroftBookofWealth.com/resources